TRANSFORMING
into DISASTER'S WORST ENEMY
UNDERNEATH THE RUBBLE

THERESA PADGETT

Transforming into Disaster's Worst Enemy!
©2021 Theresa Padgett
Published by: Theresa Padgett

ISBN: 978-0-578-96626-7
Library of Congress number: 2021915858
All rights reserved, printed in the United States of America. No part of this book may be used or reproduced in any manner whatsoever without written permission, except in the case of brief quotations embodied in reports, articles, and reviews.

Edited by: Write on Promotions
Cover: Frank Blocks Jr
Interior Layout: Write on Promotions

Dedication

In the timeframe of writing this book I went from completely broken to a place of restoration and healing. Therapeutically this book allowed me to speak from a place I never encountered before. Each page is saturated with the transparent process of realization, growth and ultimately victory all the while buried underneath the rubble. As you read this book you will hear my heart, feel my tears, see my anger, joy and laughter. I pray this book will inspire, relate and give hope to each person that it encounters. It's not by chance that you are reading this book. I want to thank my Lord and savior Jesus Christ because with man nothing is possible but with Christ all things are possible. I dedicate this book to my beautiful children Mikaylah, TJ, Anthony and Lailani who walked through this entire process with mommy and also evolved through your own personal journey. It may have been a difficult time but strenuous times will always show you what you're made out of and you, my children, are stronger than you think. My sister, Jozee, who remained in my corner loving me through this entire process. My best friend, Tiffany, encouraged me to put the first word on paper. Grateful for all of my friends, G.T's (Good Things) and family who are too many to name, but I love you all. Thank you for your prayers. I met myself for the first time and I really like her, matter of fact, I absolutely love, adore and cherish this beautiful being inside and out.

Forward

By Tiffany Holliday

To the reader of this work,

It has been my pleasure to know Theresa Padgett since the summer of 2007 when we both attended the same church. There, she taught praise dance lessons to the youth – my children included. During that summer, I learned the power and the importance of prayer, and I mustered up enough courage to ask Theresa if she would be my prayer partner and she kindly accepted. During that time, we prayed daily and held each other accountable. In a short span of time, our friendship had developed from mere acquaintance to sisterhood and partnership in ministry. I have watched her grow in her relationship with Jesus Christ to the place where her heart burns and longs to know God, be known by Him, and to make Him known. I have watched her children strive to become established as godly young people, and deeply value the contributions this family has brought to this city.

In this narrative, Theresa takes you into her world – a place of honesty, transparency, growth, grace, forgiveness, faith, spirituality, victory, identity, and humility. At her core, Theresa is a creative genius, and "transforming into disaster's worst enemy" is both poetic and inspiring. These poetic stories serve a valuable purpose and create an intensified rhythm, in which you hear the author's heartbeat. In this narrative, she takes a holistic approach with a writing style that is liberating, rejuvenating, captivating, and motivating.

You will learn from this book. You will learn the power of one's story and testimony. You will learn how God can mold you into a disaster's worst enemy. You will learn how to forgive, how to encourage and be encouraged even in the face of disaster and adversity. You will learn the power of identity - how it can cripple you when rooted in the wrong thing and immerse you in peace, love, and security when rooted in Jesus Christ.

Table of Contents

Introduction..................................…................pg 4
Baseline Health...........................…..............pg 12
Trauma……………………………………pg 34
Air (Mind)……..……………………………pg 67
Temperature(Body)..pg 77
Water(H20)(Spirit)...pg 85
Crush Syndrome……………………………pg 97
Determination……………………………..pg 107
Will to Live………………………………...pg 121
God's Will…………………………………..pg 132
Empowerment…………………………….....pg 140
About the Author…………………………..pg 147

*Transforming Into
Disasters Worst Enemy*

Introduction

The human body is so resilient. God is a genius! Once He breathed into the nostrils of Adam our DNA was programmed to fight to live through every external or internal event even if it meant until our last breath. A heart attack occurs when there is an occlusion in the blood flow via vessels by either clots or cholesterol build-up that causes death to the heart tissue. This is considered a traumatic event. In light of everything, there have been cases where there were autopsies done on people that showed a heart attack never occurred because the body miraculously grew new vessels to the portion of the heart that had a cut off of blood supply unbeknown to the person.

Over my life, I have witnessed traumatic events within the United States. Hurricane Katrina was a category 3 storm that hit Louisiana in August 2005. It was an unforgettable time for the entire world. According to the Data Center, published in July 2015, over 1,000 people died, more than a million were displaced and total damage to the area was estimated at $151 billion. There were so many heartbreaking events that occurred in the United States. There were multiple school shootings, movie theater shootings, mall shootings, grocery store shootings, public injustices and prejudices, the murder of Trevon Martin, Michael Brown, and Tamir Rice just to name a few. Daily living and the idea of the human race going about "business as usual" have been interfered with by the Boston Bomber, Charleston Church shooting and the infamous Las Vegas Mass Shooting in my very hometown. With respect to the victims, I strongly have chosen not to mention the names of these monsters and will continue to pray for the survivors and family members of the victims. I believe one of the most unforgettable events that occurred in the United States is a date that every person can tell you exactly what they were doing and where they were during this unfortunate attack and that was September 11th, 2001.

Although these incidents did not directly affect me, watching these disasters unfold affected my sense of security, mental awareness, and faith indirectly. However, that is not the case with a woman by the name of Gennelle Guzman-McMillian. This is a woman who on September 11th became a direct victim of a terrifying attack which in return turned around her faith for the better.

According to the interview with the 700 club, Gennelle told her story of how her day started out as a normal workday where she went to work at her desk job at the World Trade Center. Her office was on the 64th floor and she found herself running in the office at 8:05 am, five minutes late. She describes how she heard a loud noise and shortly thereafter having to run for her life. She described running down the staircase with a co-worker and after reaching the 13th floor hearing more rumbling around her. Her co-worker turned back around and as she bent down to take off her shoes to follow her, she heard more rumbling, darkness consumed her and dust filled the area as the walls caved in around her. She found herself with her head pinned between steel, her arms beneath her stomach and her legs crossed in an Indian style position. Gennelle could not move anything but her left arm. She described how she began to prepare to die as there was no room to turn around, move or get comfortable. How many situations in your life left you pinned with nowhere to turn, move or get comfortable? What did you do or did you do anything at all? She recalls a piece of steel that was in her side that caused her pain.

Gennelle mentions one positive thing which was that there was something or perhaps even somebody soft underneath her that relieved some of the pressure.

    Gennelle found herself reasoning with God and began to beg Him for a second chance. She leaned on the only faith that she had to believe that somebody would still rescue her as she remained in the dark and in silence. She vowed if the Lord would save her she would be a better person and would dedicate the rest of her life to serving HIM and asked for a sign. She began to hear steel and rubble moving. She heard someone ask if she could see the light. She spoke back replying that she could not see it but did see an opening above her. She took her left hand and put it up towards the hole. Someone then grabbed her hand and she heard a voice say, "Gennelle I got you, my name is Paul." Paul held her hand as the rescue workers continued to plunder through the rubble. Finally, after 27 hours of being buried alive, she heard a closer noise of rubble moving, saw dust and she then felt someone grab her shoulders and pull her up out of the rubble. She was considered to be the last survivor of 9/11. Her vision was blurry and she could not see but she recalls asking the rescue workers if they ever saw Paul but they denied ever encountering any such person. At that moment,

Gennelle was convinced that the Lord sent her an angel. She was inspired to write a book called, "Angel in the Rubble-The Miraculous Rescue."

During Gennelle's interview with the 700 club, she spoke about how she gave her life to Jesus Christ and how she now really does believe in second chances. As she was given a second chance to live. Realizing that she is not in control of her own life and it's not about her or what she wants out of life, it's about the Lord. The Lord really does have a plan and purpose for her life and to know that her purpose was not complete here on earth. The same is for us and our situations. God is in control in spite of what it may look like or even feel like at the time. When our world comes crashing down who will we put our trust in?

I ask the question; can you survive after being buried underneath the rubble? Underneath the ashes and debris of life? I'm speaking spiritually. This world can be a cruel, dark, and evil place and if we are not careful, we could fall into defeat. Dying spiritually underneath the rubble. The devil comes yet but to steal, kill and destroy. He is always on his job yet I find that sometimes we get caught slipping because of our comfort level in our own lives. How many situations have you been through where it seemed hopeless? Almost like you weren't gonna make it? Asking the question about surviving underneath the ashes of life I found myself interested in determining the physical ways people survive such circumstances.

An individual would have a greater chance of survival if they already had a good overall baseline health. If the individual already is suffering from comorbidities such as diabetes, heart disease, or respiratory disease just to name a few, their chance of survival is smaller. The next factor would include the extent of trauma that they experienced during the disaster. Any trauma that causes excessive bleeding, wounds that automatically are at risk for infection, or head injuries make it difficult for the person to endure the time needed to be rescued in a salvageable condition. I'm going somewhere because if you're listening spiritually you will hear that depending on the trauma that we are facing in life, our survival has everything to do with our overall baseline spiritual health as related to the endurance and likable state we will come up out of the trauma whole.

There are also three other important factors that increase one's chances of survival and they are water, temperature, and air. A baby has a greater chance of survival according to UK's Royal College of Pediatrics and Child Health, it is said that, in babies, up to 90% of their bodies were made up of water, acting as a "natural storage" in cases of dehydration. There have been many baby survival stories such as a six-month-old girl that was rescued from a building four days after it collapsed in the Kenyan capital, Nairobi. A person can develop vomiting or diarrhea which can result in a loss of fluids that leads to dehydration. Between the year 2003-2013 there were 2,162 deaths in the US related to dehydration according to the Guardian issue December 2013. Temperature is indirectly related to water as the body's temperature is regulated by the amount of water that is in the body. That's why a nurse will always encourage fluids when a patient has a fever. A person can get too hot or even as a result of sweating become dehydrated due to once again, a loss of fluids. Finally, the absence of air is an obvious outcome. Being that Gennelle was rescued on the 13th floor of a 110 floors building that was crumbled, is even more reason enough to know that she had a purpose to live.

    When a person is trapped under a great deal of debris, rubble, or ash, they are at risk for a condition called the crush syndrome. This occurs because of the pressure of everything on top of the victim. The person would begin to give off an increased amount of CO_2 from their lungs, suffer renal failure, shock, and a great deal of pain. If the victims are no longer audible the rescue team would use CO_2 detectors to determine if there are still bodies underneath the rubble.

Have you ever driven past a car wreck and saw the condition of the vehicle and already lost hope? Some accidents appear to clearly have no survivors but that's not always the case. While waiting to be rescued, what promotes survival, especially in a great disaster? I've found that determination, the will to live, and ultimately God's will is an intangible factor that one can't see. Just like faith, every person has their own measure within them. Most of these survivor stories no matter the race, age, or gender, all have a similar common denominator and it is either one or a combination of all three factors. Being in the nursing field, as some may have already guessed as the majority of my metaphors are related to health, many of my patients would not die until they've given up mentally. The brain is the command center of the body and once you tell yourself you are not going to make it or you're just going to die not shortly thereafter the person will die if they believe it. So it is for your spirit. If you think you are defeated you will never be victorious or if you think you don't believe you are not joined heirs with Christ you will never reap the benefits of being a child of God.

Our bodies are up against risks of disaster daily either externally or internally, fleshly or spiritually yet the Lord miraculously keeps us from encountering certain dangers but those that do touch us are already fixed fights. How many of you have gone through a fight or are going through a fight that you think or thought was going to take you out. Like grandma used to say, if you haven't just keep living.

During the development of this very book that you are holding, you will be witnessing the live process of this journey of me finding out who I really am after disaster struck my life. The walls of my life came crashing down on me and I was pinned in between disbelief, anger, bitterness, not really knowing who I was, to begin with, and on the other end, my destiny and who God says that I am. The Lord spared me from being crushed but unbeknown to me my overall spiritual health was a challenging factor. The Lord began to transform me into disaster's worst enemy underneath the ashes, rubble, and debris of life. As this book unfolds you will find that one of the most devastating times of my life equaled the most in-depth, personal, one-on-one training experiences with the Most High God. You will find how the Lord could use your most trying time to grow you up, especially if you're behind like I was. He can still use you even if you think you're unworthy. You will find how essential survival factors such as water, temperature were used in my favor to determine my outcome. Pushing through spiritual renal failure, shock, and even pain, gave me a supernatural strength, and because I was determined and had the will to live, to survive, to make it in spite of what it looked like I'm still standing. Even after that, I'm seeing that ultimately, it was God's will for me to survive so here I write.

Chapter 7
Baseline Health

Born and raised in what I would consider the ghetto of sin city. A young girl whose mother was a prostitute and father was an alcoholic. Seeing base-heads, a term used to identify those who smoked crack, was a normal ordeal. I would see children riding bikes around those walking around smoked out oblivious to the surroundings of the dangers right in our face. Drug dealers, gang bangers, crack-heads, alcoholics, and weirdos. Learned how to adapt to a broken and dysfunctional environment early.

My mother was born in California and moved to Colorado Springs, Colorado when she was around 6-7yrs old. She is a beautiful short woman with a mixture of Native American Indian and Caucasian, having thick, black coarse hair and red-tinged, olive skin. Her father was in the army and actually fought in WWII. He graduated from barber school and was a member of a baptist church in his community. He died in 1982 from pneumonia right before my second birthday. I never had the opportunity to meet him yet I would look at pictures and be amazed at how tall and handsome he was. I would always say, "My granddaddy looks like Superman!" As I'm getting older, I realize why I never had any pictures with my grandfather holding me as a baby. My mother left Colorado by foot as she hitchhiked and prostituted her way to Las Vegas, leading me to conclude that she left abruptly and urgently. This is something she had to do.

My father was a tall, dark and handsome man, born and raised in New Orleans, Louisiana who was a bar-tender. He was the baby of eight children and was definitely a mama's boy who had amazing basketball skills. They called him "HuckleBerry Hound," a nickname that demonstrated how he was a dog on the court. I was my daddy's little girl but I also remember that he was the discipliner in the home. I recall one time in kindergarten my friends convinced me to come over to their home to play out the video, "Cool it now" by New Edition. My goodness, talk about a chance of a lifetime! I knew that mother would be meeting me at the entrance of the apartments once school let out but I figured if I could just go over there really quick and get this video done I could get back before she missed me. So without delay, I went over to the house and if anybody can recall in the video there were girls coupled up with New Edition as they have smoothly sung "Cool it now" in their 80's gear. Ralph Tresvant was undeniably my favorite! Here we were all coupled up rehearsing the scene with the door wide open when like lightning a black and white patrol car pulls up. Out of the back seat came a tall, dark, handsome but yet irritated 6-foot brother who literally did not say a mumbling word to me. My father looked at me and pointed. I walked hastily to the car and got in the backseat. We didn't even have a video recorder...some friends! When we got back to the apartment it must have been the talk of our complex because neighbors began to run up asking if everything was alright. I recall my dad saying she's fine and the last thing I remember before the infamous leather therapy, known as a butt whooping, was my friend's mother's face before him, shutting the door, saying, "Joe, don't whoop her."

    No matter how many spankings I received, there was nothing you could tell me bad about my daddy. I looked for him to walk through the door everyday. He was a good father to me but I noticed a few things about him that weren't so good. My father was a bonafide functional alcoholic. His drink of choice was Hennessy and I noticed it to be wherever he was. He would drink from 4:30 am until 4:29 am if you get my drift. He was shot in his shoulder at the

Theresa Padgett

bar that he worked at and it made a few of his fingers on the right hand slightly but noticeably contracted. The reason why I remember that hand is because he would always have his bottle of Hennessy in it, and yes, he drank right out of the bottle. He carried the bottle in his right back jeans pocket wherever he went. Yet he still maintained his responsibility as he got up every day and went to work, kept food in the house, and a roof over our head. He was a fighter and a visible protector of the home. I saw him chase down a man on the heart of the westside who stole my mother's purse and brought it back to her after he did God-knows-what to retrieve it. My aunt told me that my parents met during the time she was hitchhiking to Las Vegas. My dad worked at a motel she stopped by and he allowed her to live there for a while free of charge or not. She ended up pregnant with me and my dad vowed to never leave her and to take care of his responsibility which was me. This was five years after his marriage ended and his ex-wife, a beautiful woman, left and took their five children and returned to Louisiana. My mother never had to work; however, he was very abusive to her. I would hear her crying, yelling, and screaming as I would witness him choking or hitting her at the dining room table. Never did I say anything, and quite frankly, I don't ever remember how any of those scenes played out. I believe this is where the unfortunate blocking of serious life situations and the inability to process tragic events would have begun in my life.

My mother loved the Lord and I recall her being the only white woman I saw living on the Westside of Las Vegas where it was predominantly only a black community. There was never a Sunday where we were not in a baptist church. I would find myself enjoying real Sunday school, which we have gotten away from, and a period of my mother enjoying the choir as she rocked back and forth, clapping off beat and singing in loud, non-detailed oriented words and obnoxious singing voice. I can laugh about it as I can admit that singing is not my gift either. My dad would drop us off in his tan Cadillac and be in the parking lot full of alcohol, at the end of service to take us home. The above events, listening to Michael Jackson's beat it record, and watching PBS television seemed to be my normal lifestyle until my life was forever changed abruptly.

When I was 7yrs old my adult cousin came to the house during a time when my father abruptly stopped coming home. She told my mother, as per my aunt, that it was close to the summer and she wanted me to come to her house to stay with her and her kids to give my mom a break. Come to find out it was

Theresa Padgett

actually March-April, my father was in the hospital and the family was concerned that my mother was not capable of taking care of me on her own. I thank God it happened because I had no respect for my mother and she could barely take care of herself. I would have been a menace to society with no respect for authority. I saw my dad treat her bad so I would treat her bad when he was not around. I talked back, sassed her, and would never listen to what she would tell me to do. She would wait for him to come home and tell my father what I did like a sibling would, then I would get in trouble. I remember my mother told me to go run some bath water and take my bath one night. I peeked in the room and saw my dad lying in the bed with his eyes closed, then I slowly frowned my eyebrows, cut my eyes and said "No." My dad had to be a superhero because I never saw a belt appear so fast. Needless to say, by the time I got in the tube, bath-time turned into a place of refuge. After staying a couple of weeks with my cousin, she called me over to her one day when her son and I were outside playing. She called me into the house with tears in her eyes as I noticed her fumbling with words. She was sitting and pulled me close to her as she held my wrists. She told me that my father was in the hospital and that he died, then she grabbed me close and began crying harder. I don't remember crying nor what I did after I heard the news. Once again, an example of me blocking out a tragic event. The funeral was like attending church service, yet I saw my father in the center, on top of a low seated stage in a white casket. He looked like he was sleeping. I remember looking around at my surroundings and noticed all of my family members crying and comforting one another. They would look at me with compassion in their eyes and whisper "I'm sorry" and "It's ok" to me as so many people were smothering me with hugs but yet I don't remember crying. I walked up to the casket in my all yellow dress and stared at his face. I can recall seeing a tear on his cheek perfectly displaced as if he had cried it out himself, but yet I don't remember crying.

    My father was working at a local hotel at the time of his death and had great benefits. He was part of the Culinary union, and at the time of his death, my family received a nice lump sum to bury him and take care of his affairs. My cousin would not return me to my mother, and after I grew up, I read some court papers that revealed that the family was afraid for my well-being as she was prostituting. She went back to what she knew because my father was the main source of income. Likewise, no matter what we are delivered from, we, as a people, are always threatened by the possibility of returning to what we were delivered from when faced with life circumstances, especially if our faith is not anchored in the Lord. We can't just attend church as a ritual or tradition and never really accept the true transformation of Jesus Christ through the gospel. As believing in the Father, although we fight with our flesh daily, the relationship should be evident in the fruit that we bear in this thing called life.

Not long after the funeral, my cousin called me over as she sat in the same chair that she revealed about my father's death and asked me if I wanted to go to my uncle's home to stay or child haven. Looking up at her with a confused face, I remember my uncle, my dad's older brother, who was a tall man, average 6 ft. tall as my father was but he had this deep, mean, raspy Barry White voice. "No, ma'am, I will take Child Haven, please," I responded. I was terrified of my uncle. Child Haven is a licensed shelter in the Clark County area that houses a maximum of 90 children who cannot safely remain with their families. Not really processing what Child Haven was, I found myself having my bath time coordinated, an organized dinner, and bunking in a room of 2 other children. My mother came to visit me once and I noticed she was pregnant. After the short visitation she left and I don't remember crying. My uncle told me after I got older that he ran across my mother on the streets and she ran over to him to tell him that I was in Child Haven and she could not get me out. My uncle told me as my father was on his dying bed that he looked him in his eyes and told him no matter what happened to him, make sure to take care of me. My uncle, who I refused to live with, immediately began the process of adoption. A man and his wife who already raised four of their own children, whose baby was already 19 years old, so unselfishly welcomed me in their home and treated me as their very own child. They both worked the labor of gruesome hotel jobs. I say that as per my experience was really difficult. The hotel was easy work when you've been in the country picking cotton since you were a child. That is one of the reasons my family migrated here to Vegas. They worked hard until they retired with the effects of back pain, arthritis, etc…They allowed me to talk to my mother as often as she wanted to call. From a mature standpoint, I thank the Lord that they brought me into their home as I could have been adopted by strangers and would have never known my family.

    I was quiet, timid, and scared. I remained in front of the television, sitting Indian style for a great period of my life. Wasn't used to eating anything but canned soups and fried chicken. My aunt would cook like we were in the country on a daily basis. There was not one dinner meal that I had that did not include homemade cornbread and she cooked everyday. That's one benefit of being from the dirty south...you're going to eat.

There was a Methodist church that literally sat in the desert, two houses down from our home. I begged my aunt and uncle to take me. They did not attend church but permitted me to walk over every Sunday. I would get dressed up nice and pretty then truck across the desert, getting my patent-leather shoes dusty every Sunday. I joined the children's choir, knowing I couldn't sing, but I enjoyed the fellowship and felt like I belonged to something. We learned memory verses, had fashion shows and participated in plays. Yes, all by myself, I had the wherewithal to remain dedicated. I even joined the usher ministry. I remained in that church until I got in high school and began to put God on the back burner.

I was always on lock down because my aunt and uncle did not want to allow the streets to get me as it had affected their children's lives. I would watch my friends walk down the street until I found myself creating ideas to interest them into coming over. We would play basketball with a trash can and soccer ball, play dominoes in the front yard, or even make-up

Transforming Into Disasters Worst Enemy

dances. I loved to dance as it took me away from my reality. I grew up around people who had an addiction to crack cocaine and that drug was a monster. I would find homemade crack pipes under the coffee tables or hidden in the couch, made out of the cardboard on pant hangers and copper mesh dish pot scrubs. There would be this slow, thick smoke present at times when the door opened and the smell was a distinct sweet yet potent stitch that only one would have to smell to relate to as they walked out with bucked glossy eyes. Any money or clothes with a tag on them would be stolen if the tag was not removed. I remember keeping money in between my mattress and finding myself rising in the bed while asleep as folks searched my room in the middle of the night for money. I used to watch helplessly as my uncle would chase his sons out of the house with a loaded 12-gauge shotgun gun after being confronted about my aunts missing purse or wallet. I would hide crouched low on the side of the securely locked D-freezer which had the fish and steaks, those things that were easily sold. Sharing this experience is not to hurt the ones I love but only speak from a young girl's eyes. Crazy times but thank God for deliverance now.

    At the age of 9yrs old, I had the opportunity of meeting my five siblings that left Las Vegas with their mother before I was born. It was bitter and sweet because I was apprehensive about meeting new people yet was excited that I wasn't an only child. They stood around me in a circle and stared at me with almost disbelief on their faces. No one spoke or made any gestures at me, showing any interest, acceptance, rejection, or emotion. After a couple of years, my big sister moved to Las Vegas whom I ended up living with in my 11th-12th grade year. They all slowly traveled to Vegas, some stayed and some went back to the south. They all welcomed me as their sister, and to this day, we all have phenomenal relationships as if we grew up together under the same roof. Once again, if my dad's brother never adopted me would I have known them? The Lord was looking out for me before I could even acknowledge who He was.

    I recall being confused about my identity at an early age. Growing up in an all-black family and in a black neighborhood, I never felt as if I really belonged. Always looking around, I never saw anybody that looked like me. Nobody's mother looked or behaved like mine. Therefore, I remained in continuous embarrassment about having a white/native American mother. It was such an uncommon reality in my world. I didn't want anybody connecting me to her. Why would this happen to me? It was almost as if the union of my parents was taboo, it shouldn't have happened. Should I even exist? I remember pulling my best friend to the side at school in the 6th grade, examining the room for ear hustlers so I could tell her the greatest secret in my life. After making this revealing of my secret the main event, I looked my friend in the face as I clutched my sweaty palms, took a deep breath and said, "I'm not all the way black. My mother is white and I am mixed." My friend looked me in the eyes and said, "I know." And we went back to the playground as if nothing ever happened. Children are undeniably pure in spirit and non-judgmental. Mark 10:15 reads, "Truly, I say to you, whoever does not receive the kingdom of God like a child shall not enter it." Children represent a spiritual posture that we should uphold as we serve our Father in heaven.

    I found myself getting lost in dance as I got older. I would find dance teams to join at our local recreation center, Doolittle Community Center. There was an Arts Center that taught African Dance, Ballet, and Hip hop. I joined groups that didn't require much parent participation. Matter of fact, my aunt and uncle never knew what I could do. All of my friends had family at each event but my aunt and uncle never saw any of my performances. I didn't let it affect me as the excitement from being on the stage with the light blinding me took away from me seeing the faces of the people. I personally know how important it is to keep these programs up and running as it saved me from an array of devastating possibilities. I remember the times I would lallygag walking home from school or get out of the house before my aunt and uncle came home, under the direction of my cousin, with the agreement that I took her daughters with me. Being free was worth the extra babysitting gig. However, when out, the very world was trying to soak me up into its very trap. I had an older homeboy who sat me at the park bench one day and pulled his gun out, placed it in my hands, and began telling me how to shoot it. There was a time when these same guys would have me and my best friend randomly beat up, chicks to so call "quote" them in the local neighborhood gang. It was crazy because we did nothing to earn our place in it; however, because our uncles and brothers were a part of the gang, it was almost as if we were grandfathered in. Our favorite color was purple, so I was told, and we found ourselves wearing it almost every day. We really thought we were something but if some real gangsta would have brought that heat we would have cried like two helpless children.

On the other side, the Lord was working an alternate route, I found time to join a drill team when

Transforming Into Disasters Worst Enemy

I was 13 years old. I learned that I had no rhythm in this era of my life. Those who know me today as a choreographer of many groups, a dancer, and a performing arts workshop director literally do not believe me. The drill team marked the start of me finding my tempo as we only marched to the sounds of ten snares and bass drums. This is where I met the man who ended up being my husband of 17 years and the father of three of my children. Just a few hours a week our young black boys on the westside were able to drift away from their reality as they gave their all and rocked the drums. We had a little crush on each other that did not amount to a hill of beans because we were kids. We found out we were better as friends and I found myself confiding in him about my relationships and trying to hook him up with other girls as we got older. More about that later.

I signed up for a dance class at my local high school to obtain credit. This is where I was totally shell-shocked. There was more to dancing than just hip hop! Although it was out of my comfort zone I found myself enjoying the different volumes of dance. I ended up taking that class over 2 years of my high school career. It was here where I learned a touch of jazz, contemporary and liturgical dance. A group of my friends and myself found a really cool teacher, Ms.

Theresa Padgett

Johnson, to stay after school with us to support our very own self-grown dance group called "X-Posse." We were permitted to dance during all of the assemblies and would kill the cheerleader's performance with our crazy sexy cool routines. Simultaneously, during this time a man from the Alpha Phi Alpha fraternity, who happens to be my homegirl's uncle, decided he was going to start a boy and girl youth group at the Doolittle community center. It was also in my freshman year, my sisters and I became the blueprint of DphiT (Divas of Tomorrow) who is still fully functioning within the community. My older sister would come to performances but otherwise, I would have no one else unless she invited them.

    In the 11th grade, I ended up leaving the nest and moving in with her. I came to a point where the over-the-top ways of discipline began to put anger and rage in my heart. Although it was not an everyday occasion, I began to understand that the pulling of my hair, telling me how ugly I was and all I have is hair, the pouring beer on me and crazy slaps in the face, whooping with belts and switches were only a product of my families upbringing and it was not going to change. I love my people but if we could only learn that how mama and them used to do it don't make it right. We are so stuck in tradition as a people that as sheep we can find ourselves falling over a cliff if we don't choose our own way. Therefore, being connected to the Divas was very difficult to let go of as I had finally had sisters who accepted me. Well, a few were catty, but this was my new world. I completely agree with my Kingdom-driven community on the revelation of how sororities and fraternities are servants of other gods. I believe it served its purpose of teaching me sisterhood without tainting my belief system and I thank God it wasn't as intense as the college level.

 I went through many changes during this time of my life. On top of a dysfunctional family dynamic, never being hugged or having a voice I never really felt like I belonged. I really wanted to die and used to make comments like, "I wish I was dead," "I don't know why I'm here." I'm so glad the Lord did not take my life. I remember running away from home at the age of 13. My sister and other aunt spent tireless hours and days searching for me. My aunt and uncle, from my knowledge, never physically looked for me but did call the police. When I returned home the police was in my living room and made it clear that the law states that I had to live there until I turned 18 years old. At that moment, I remember the little demon of anger that I dealt with ended up being a full-grown spirit of rebellion. I was completely against everything and wanted to hurry up and grow up. I always just wanted to go. Side note, whenever I don't like something I'd rather just go. I didn't have to endure the stress anymore. My focus was on getting a job at 16yrs old and getting up out of that house. Although I did start working at 16yrs, I couldn't last until age 18. I wasn't an angel and I never blatantly disobeyed them but I did find a way to do it behind their back. I had a sassy little mouth at times but would spit the majority of my venom under my breath but loud enough for my aunt to know that I did say something. Other than dance and listening to music, there was nowhere for me to get this anger out. I felt like I was in prison, waiting for my time to be served. So adapting, ignoring my reality, and avoiding how I felt became my way of life. Hey, I couldn't change it, and having a voice meant I thought I was grown, so it didn't exist in my head. Unfortunately, I brought those abnormal coping mechanisms into my adulthood as you will find out later.

    When I was in the 11th grade around the age of 17, my aunt slapped me because of my smart mouth and as I began to block my face with my arms I accidentally hit her somewhere and she lost it. She poured her beer on top of my head and called me all types of "bitches." When my uncle came home I knew he would understand my plea as I did not intentionally mean to hit her. He came into the room, did not care to hear my side of the story, and slapped me in my face. He had only spanked me one time before that and that was when I was 9 years old. My heart was broken that he did not even consider my side of the story but what did I expect, I never had a voice. His wife would do all the discipline because he was never home. He would leave the house for work and end up coming home after or right before I went to bed because of his after-hour street activities. I remember screaming that I was leaving and I hated him. He punched a gigantic hole in my wall. I scurried down to my other aunt's house and called my sister and we ended up going back to the house to obtain the rest of my clothing because, at that moment, I knew my uncle had given up on me. They didn't even fight to keep me, how disappointing.

    After enduring a life where I learned how to adapt to my home and neighborhood. The environment of drive-by shootings, drug activity, physical, mental abuse, dysfunctional relationships, borderline poverty, and death my sister brought me to a calm, functional reality. It was so peaceful that I almost was afraid to believe it. Unfortunately, I still brought those coping skills and rebellion. I was angry and insensitive as I never remember anybody hugging me, kissing my forehead, or making my voice important. I remember I would go to the back room when adults would come over as my aunt would make it clear that kids are to be seen and not heard. Without any effort, I graduated with a "C" average as my aunt and uncle would push me to only graduate. I never thought we could have an opportunity to go to college as little black children from the west side. Nobody from my block went to college until I looked across the street and saw a glimpse. I had a cousin who graduated one year before me who actually enrolled in UNLV to become a teacher. It was unbelievable, if she could do it I could do it too but what do I want to be other than a hotel employee. She now is an excelling school teacher with her master's degree. It's so funny, she uses our favorite past-time street game, domino, as one of the most effective learning tools within her classroom. I absolutely love this girl, she is one of the very few teachers that I know who is compassionate and serious about what they do. I wasn't sure what I wanted to be but I knew what I wasn't going to be. That was broke, an addict, or a hotel employee.

    Finally, after graduating high school in June, I accomplished getting my very own apartment by September in my name but with my boyfriend. I enrolled in community college to work towards a nursing degree as my ASVAB test ruled out that I would be good at helping people. My big sister got me a job at the hotel she was working at because I lost my job at the Greyhound bus station and I had already had the responsibility of bills and rent. I had to do something I vowed never to do as an adult but when it's either that or the streets you got to take a deep breath and make it happen. I can't deny, I was making the most money that I ever made in my life but I hated the way the hotel smelled. I couldn't get used to the wall of smoke I had to walk through as it reminded me of how my home was. There was so much smoke in my home on a daily basis that I am grateful that I did not inquire about any diseases related to second-hand smoke. I went to school reeking of smoke in my clothes and my hair. It was so embarrassing but I still had to push through. My sister didn't realize that, by this time, I was a couple of months pregnant with my oldest daughter at the tender age of 18. The cleaning supplies were killing me. The physical labor of bending, pulling, and getting on my knees to clean tubes in a minimum of 15 rooms a day was unbearable. How could my aunt do this for almost 40 years? I was on the city bus and had to keep a bag on me to vomit as I was in a continuous state of nausea. After about 2 weeks, I quit my job and my sister was livid as she put her neck on the line to get me hired.

When she found out I was pregnant it broke my heart to see how disappointed she was. I knew I had to figure something out in order to take care of this baby. I ended up enrolling in CSN for nursing and getting a job at Footlocker but by this time, my boyfriend of 2 years became extremely abusive and I was in too deep to get out. He would have girls in the house, man-handle, hit, and choke me. He would publicly humiliate me and disrespect me even in front of his mother and sister. He knocked me out one day in my living room in front of one of his friends. I remember him locking the door so his friend could not stop him and the last thing I remember was his friend climbing through the window. I woke up on the floor with him yelling, raging, and spitting in my face as his homeboy was trying to calm him down. Another time, we were at the downtown bus exchange and I remember blacking out but still being conscious enough to hear him. We weren't fighting but I believe it was the result of the abuse I endured. It was the most frightening day ever because I thought my sight was not going to return. He was very jealous, possessive, and angry. What's sad is that I never believed that I was in an abusive relationship because being from the hood, somewhere in my messed up head, I believed that when I fought back it negated the fact that it was still abuse. I went to my aunt and uncle's house with a black eye, after mending our relationship with the invitation to my high school graduation, and sobbed as my uncle laughed about my eye being black and swollen. He said, "Oh, he hit you in the eye huh?" I felt naked, unprotected, and embarrassed. My aunt tried to comfort me by sharing her story that my uncle used to abuse her until she pushed him in the closet and hit him with a plate of eaten neck bones while he was drunk. Ok, I see why they thought it was ok. They were still together but something down inside of me would not let me accept that this was supposed to be the way life should be. I was estranged from all of my friends, and as I went through the process of this abuse, I would only tell my sister so much. I would only call her when I proclaimed it was over and I wanted to come live with her. Me and my baby would pack up about 4-5 times to come to her until she finally told me if I was going to keep going back not to come. My two older brothers, who were in Vegas, could never find his whereabouts until I decided to go back, and because of my poor decision, felt it would be useless if I was going to keep going back. My older sister also suffered abuse in Louisiana and my brothers used to deal with her abuser but she would end up returning to the chaos. They were fed up and it wasn't until she left the state of Louisiana to get away from him that they took her seriously. It was awkward but interesting how generational curses tend to follow down the line until someone has the courage to break it.

Chapter 2
Trauma

This was a very dark and cloudy time for me. Talk about walking through the valley of the shadow of death. The Lord truly was my rod and my staff. During my pregnancy, there was not much pressure released from the pain and drama in my life. My daughter's father, who was 17yrs old, decided he was going to gamble while at work and ended up losing his job. We were now two teenagers in an apartment that we could not afford. We ended up getting evicted and he moved in with his mother and I moved in with my Godmother. Little background on my Godmother, she was a narcissistic, ex-gangbanger who was introduced into the family after she was a roommate of my older cousin in the penitentiary. She charmed her way into our family when I was around 11 years old but I absolutely loved her because once again I found a sense of belonging in her family. She would buy me gifts, take me to her house and treat me as her own child. Although she had 6 children of her own she brought me into her life because I resembled her children and she would claim me to everyone she knew. To be honest, when out in public no one could tell us apart. Her oldest daughter was about 3 years younger than me and she was already by this time going down the wrong path as she was always fighting and getting kicked out of school. When I moved in with them, I was four months pregnant, lost, unstable, yet would not stop going to school. I quickly changed from a registered nurse to a medical assistant as the completion time was only 6-10 months and I had to be stable by the time my baby was born. I mean, I figured they wore scrubs and had a stethoscope as well. I'm sure the pay was the same? I remember one day being in the house around 9 pm. There was a knock on the door and after one of the kids answered it and informed the person that whom he was looking for did not reside at that address he returned again. This time the kids came and got me and asked me to answer the door since I was the oldest. I answered the door but no one said anything, I opened the door and saw a young guy about my age standing next to his car in the driveway. He said, "What's up?" A few times and looking confused, I said, " I'm sorry I don't know you, you must have me confused with my God-sister as we did look alike, I turned around to grab her as I glanced back while grabbing the door to close it. The man from a distance raised his right arm and began to shoot

Transforming Into Disasters Worst Enemy

several rounds of the 9milimiter gun in his hand. Immediately I felt as if time had stopped and I was encased in this bubble as the wind of the bullets flying past my ears sounded as if we were under water. I was literally moving in slow motion as I fell to the ground to crawl to safety. The bullets were hitting the door and other areas of the house. This person then proceeded to walk around the perimeter of the house shooting out windows and the backyard sliding glass door. I remember eventually reaching the master bedroom closet laying prostrate on the floor praying that God would just let me live. Once the bullets ceased, my Godmother brought us all to the living room and as we waited for the police to get there we prayed on the floor. After the police completed their investigation, I called my daughter's father and he sent me a cab to come to his mother's house. My Godmother was so upset with me. She told me if I could not stay with them as a family that night she would disown me and I was to never come back. She had no compassion over the fact that I almost lost my and my baby's life. There was no sense of security in the home, I was trembling and the only way to get some peace was to leave. So, I left and it was all downhill from there with our relationship. I remember coming back to the home to get my clothes, we argued, emotions were high, she and her daughter tried to fight me. Our relationship was over and to the point of no return, as I left and vowed to never look back. I still don't remember crying about the rejection and hurt that I experienced. She died about 7 years later from breast cancer. We did, however through the grace of God, have an opportunity to make amends as I heard she was sick and reached out to her. She invited me over and we cried, talked, apologized to one another and I was able to enjoy her life for just a little while longer. Time is the most precious gift anyone can give you. It is priceless because no matter how hard we pray we can never get back the last day, week, hour, minute, or second that has already been spent. There are no refunds, no do-overs or repeats. It was about another month or so before the Lord called her home. This time, I do remember crying. Forgiveness not only sets the one who needs forgiveness free but it sets the forgiver free.

  Still pregnant with my first child, I was working diligently to complete the medical assistant program. I recall walking several miles every day, hopping walls, and catching buses tirelessly as I doubled up and took both night and day classes and still maintained a job. We were living with his parents and I was still working at the Foot Locker. I've always been a go-getter and once my mind is focused on something it will be completed by any means necessary. Who else is going to look out for me but me? I could never return to my aunt or my Godmother. I wanted my sister to believe me when I said I was ready to be on my own; therefore, I felt as if I had no other choice but to make it happen. Failure was never an option although the abuse was still present with my daughter's father.

    We had our own apartment and vehicle by the time I gave birth to my beautiful daughter, and here I was, with a baby to show love to and wasn't even sure what love looked like. Yet, I knew when I looked in her eyes, I had somebody else who was depending on me not to fail and I had more than myself to live for. My plan of completing the program before she came into this world did not work however I did not give up. So, needless to say, after 2 weeks of giving birth I had to make my way back to work so we could survive. I was working a job with no benefits, PTO time nor did I have any other means of income.

    At the end of July during monsoon season, I returned to work at Foot Locker while I continued chipping away at my Medical Assistant degree. My aunt kept my baby on the west side of town. During this season, the clouds were lower than usual and lightning

Theresa Padgett

would strike closer to the ground than one would be comfortable with. This year, there were several reports of casualties from lightning strikes such as trees setting on fire, houses being set on fire, people were riding their motorcycles and would get hit by lightning. One particular night around 9 pm as I was driving to pick up my daughter, the road only had one lane going north and one lane going south. I was traveling north in my dark blue 5.0 mustang with the 5-star rims jamming to legendary Mya and Method man on the radio. I faintly remember seeing a rig truck coming towards me in oncoming traffic to my left side when all of a sudden it immediately transformed into 10 am, simultaneously I heard a loud volt and it felt as if my car was hit by another vehicle. As quickly as it flashed 10 am my world returned to 9 pm and my car was in the left lane facing oncoming traffic. It took me a minute to realize that I was on the wrong side of the road. It was raining lightly, the road was clear in both directions and after reality hit, I hurried to return my vehicle to the correct lane as I lingered in confusion. I parked the car on the side of the road to collect my thoughts. After sitting for a short time I placed the vehicle in drive and was unable to pull off. As the motor revved up, I could not get it to move. I was not going to be able to go anywhere. I then ran into the first door I saw what happened to be a local bar. Without delay, they turned my young 19-year-old self around, declaring I was too young to be in there no matter the tears and look of fear in my eyes. They told me to use the payphone outside and there was no way I would pick up a phone and dial out in the rain. I kept going into bars and finally, someone had compassion enough to let me use their phone. After calling my daughter's father who assured me he was on his way I took a look at the hood of my car and noticed a hole that was an estimated diameter of a quarter or 50 cent piece. After the mechanic looked at it several days later he told us that the hole had actually penetrated all the way through from the top to the bottom of the transmission. It wasn't until I was in my 30's when I was preparing to speak before God's people that He told me to use this testimony. The nugget that the Lord wanted me to drop on His people was this, Matt 24:27, "For as lightning that comes from the east is visible even in the west, so will be the coming of the Son of Man." The lightning struck my vehicle so fast that I didn't have time to scream, ask God for forgiveness, brace myself, or anything, and just as quickly as the lightning came and caused damage as quickly as we can lose our lives. Choose ye this day on whom you are going to serve.

Theresa Padgett

As time continued the ups and downs of this relationship wore me out but yet it was creating a monster. I accepted a great deal of abuse from my car windshield getting busted out while I was trying to reverse my car, us arguing in front of his friends and family, running from him, being knocked out cold, not to mention him kicking me out of the car while 8-9 months pregnant and making me walk several miles home. The list goes on and on. He would carry out these acts in front of his mother and sister. His baby sister would stick up for me. The man had no respect for his mother and it was obvious as when I would visit when we were 16-17yr old him and his mother would be sharing a 40oz of beer. It was no different from the house I grew up in. My folks would offer me cans of beer at 7 years old. I would go into the bathroom, pour half down the drain and act like I was drinking it. I hate the taste and smell of beer to this day. The positive thing was that I found that survival was a choice and it took resilience to overcome and the power of God to endure. Negatively, the coping skills I learned as a child may have kept me in this relationship, and others to come in this story a lot longer than the Lord may have intended. I can block out an entire war zone around me and study for a test. You're not hearing me… I can knit on a leaking boat that is in stormy, furious waters.

Transforming Into Disasters Worst Enemy

Some may look at this as a good thing because I don't react to trouble as many would but it can also be a very dangerous place. I found that just because I didn't acknowledge that I was dying didn't negate the fact that I was dying slowly. Instead of removing the spiritual killer's hand from my mouth as I suffocated, I placed my hand over his hand as if he wasn't there. Only assisting him in my demise. Ignoring red flags and the obvious threat to my well-being did not make me strong, it made me careless and as quiet as it's kept....disobedient. The effects of my reality still were present even though I gave it no credit. I could probably write an entire book on the many testimonies the Lord have given me but that will come in the near future. One thing I do know, if you allow the Lord to fight your battles you will be victorious in the end. He will truly make your enemies your footstool and the silent voice of peace and success will speak loudness of revenge for you.

    Just want to thank those who spoke against me, those who said I couldn't do it, and, most of all, those who tried to hold me back. You were the fuel that I needed that set the fire under my feet to get me to run faster towards my destiny! I would have never saved my money to buy my first car if I didn't see my daughter's father drive past me at 5 am in the mornings on his way home from leaving the night before while I was at the bus stop to take my baby to the babysitters, then go to work for 8 am. Nah, I would have never decided to go back to college if a man never showed me that I should never depend on anybody else, I needed to get myself in a position to be able to take care of me and my daughter no matter who would or would not be there. My haters pushed me closer to the Lord, degraded me to my knees in prayer, betrayed me forward to trust in the Lord with all my heart, and ridiculed me towards heavenly places. This relationship made me realize what I did not want in a man. During this time, I reestablished my relationship with Jesus Christ. My aunt and sister joined a non-denominational church that I later visited and found the word of God to be so profound. Our Pastor, a young man in his 30's, was on fire and I could understand every word he was saying. I became hungry for the word of God and I was reborn again. The church began in the multipurpose room at an elementary school but it wasn't the building that kept me. I was learning and motivated to read the bible. I wanted to know more about Jesus. Once they moved to an actual location my family and I went with them. I found myself getting stronger and stronger but it wasn't external. One day my Pastor said something to me that was life-changing

Transforming Into Disasters Worst Enemy

but yet so simple. He told the congregation, "People will only treat you how you let them." I know that sounds like common sense but I needed to hear that. I guess if I had my father, this would have been the ideal time that I would need his wisdom. Although my father abused my mother I never felt like he was a monster. My mother never fought back, therefore, I didn't think I was being abused because I would always fight back. We were just fighting physically and in some twisted area of my mind, it wasn't abuse. But God does not intend on us to live that way. He said that "I come that you may have life and that more abundantly."

When was I going to ever choose an abundant life? My daughter and I continued to go to church but when I went home nothing would change. One night, when my baby was 18 months old, we came home around 11:30 pm and immediately my phone rang. On the other end was my daughter's dad and he began to question me about where I was all night and no matter how true the explanation I had explained me being with my family he ended the call abruptly with, "I'm gonna whoop your ass when I get home." I hung up and dozed off to sleep. The Holy Spirit woke me up at 2 am and told me loud and clear to go get the gun out of the closet and hide it. I was terrified of guns but I mustered up enough courage to go dig it out of the closet and I threw it under the mattress. I laid back and was able to fall back asleep. This time I was startled by the punch to my temple that was delivered by my child's father. I jumped up and immediately began to fight back. As he was getting the best of me I saw the iron on the ironing board in my peripheral view on the right side of the room. I ran over, grabbed the iron, wrapped the cord around my arm, and began to whack him as many times as I could with the iron. At this point, I was making him more and more mad. He began to rage even worse and ran to the closest to retrieve his gun. He yelled, "Where's my gun!" I told him that I got rid of it because I had already had a conversation with him that I did not want it in the house. He was so angry as he started tearing up the room in a desperate search for this weapon. He then went to the right side of the bed while I stood helplessly on the left side. He grabbed the mattress and lifted it up, then right before my eyes, I witnessed this extra-heavy piece of steel lift up as if it was attached to the mattress, and seconds before he dropped the mattress, he glanced away, the gun fell and the mattress dropped on top of it. He never saw the gun. My heart was in my bladder as I continued to yell that it was gone. I couldn't believe that the thought actually crossed his mind and that he would consider shooting me. I ran to the living room where my baby stood in her diaper afraid and all alone. We had round glass end tables and a round glass coffee table with marble bases. He took the glass from one of the small tables and threw it forcefully into the middle of the coffee table and thick glass shattered all over the living room. My baby was so scared that she couldn't even cry until I picked her up. Fear literally took her breath. I picked her up and as she cried to the top of her lungs, I vowed that we were done with this life and we were going to be free.

    The Lord will always give you a way out. After my heart was set on freedom, that's all I saw. It's never easy when you want change. When you turn around, it literally feels like a magnet is pulling you closer and closer to the way of life you were used to due to comfortability. When you are ok with being out of the zone of comfort, the Lord can then have HIS way. I remember praying and asking God to make it easy, it was time to go. It just so happens that during the time of that tragic event with the gun, my lease was up, and although fearful to live alone, I knew I could not live with him anymore. God's ways are not our ways and His thoughts are not our thoughts. Let me tell you how wise the Lord is. We packed up all of our things and my daughter's father and his friends moved all of our belongings to the new apartment. All of his clothes, shoes, and belongings were stacked up in boxes near the closet. While unpacking my daughter's and my things he looked at me and said you need to unpack my stuff by the time I get back or I'm going to my mother's house. I thought to myself, Lord, are You really going to make it this easy? So of course, I tested the waters. It wasn't long that night that he returned and headed straight to see if I did what he told me to do. He looked at his stuff and without delay believing he was punishing me, grabbed all of his unpacked items and took them to his car. He marched to the car and in a defiant voice vowed he was not returning. I was so excited! Free at last, free at last, thank God almighty I'm free at last!

  Now came the cocoon part of my life. I had to learn how to readjust my norm. Realizing my codependency in having a man in the house and never living on my own brought a choking feeling of fear. This began my process of true independence. I was such a scary cat. I would sleep with all the lights on, a couch behind the front door, my bedroom door shut with a dresser behind it, and under my pillow was a faithful old butcher knife. Not realizing if a fire broke out or an emergency happened in my bedroom I would have been domed. Continuing my walk in Christ, I began to see the Lord as my strength and my source. It was a constant battle because even though he wanted me to suffer it wasn't long before he began to speak sweet nothings in my ear again. This time my mind was made up and I would not give in. His words slowly turned from sweet to hate. He then began to call, bragging on his new past-time of pimping. The more he realized it was over between me and him the further away he pulled from our daughter. Visiting her less and neglecting to provide for her. It was all good because I already prepared myself not to depend on anybody but me and the Lord. I remember one day as he had her in a terrible neighborhood, something told me to go pick her up. I called him to find out his whereabouts and told him I was on my way. The few times he would pick her up I would find that it wasn't long before he would leave her with someone so he could selfishly continue doing his own thing. I didn't mind his mother or sister but when he would start leaving her with chicks that were prostituting for him or his homeboy's girlfriends, it became a little uneasy. After showing up, I found my baby in the house with his homeboy's chick, I grabbed her and walked to the car. He was outside and because I would not give him the time of day he became angry and we started to argue. I had my sister and cousin in the car and they kept telling me to stop arguing and just get in the car. My daughter and I got into the back seat and before we got about 12 feet away, he pulled out a gun and began shooting. I honestly don't know if he was shooting in the air or if he was shooting at the vehicle but my cousin began to drive recklessly back and forth in every attempt to avoid contact with any bullet. Yet, I noticed as my daughter, sister and I were being tossed back and forth in our seats my sweet cousin who strongly resembles the beautiful Janet Jackson pulled out her gun with her right hand and pointed out of her window only deciding in the spare of the moment not to pull the trigger which would have placed us in the back seat in more danger. We got out of there alive but not without the crippling reality that once again this man has shown no regard for not only my life but our very own daughter's life.

    Over time, this man stopped coming around so often or even calling. In my maturity, I decided at a young age not to be the one to make anyone be a father and it was him that was going to develop his own relationship with his daughter. He would use excuses that he was broke and didn't want to come and see her without any money or that he didn't have anything to bring to her. I would counteract his every attempt to validate his rejection, explaining that she did not even know how to count therefore she could care less what he had in his pocket or hand to give her. But there was no convincing him. Eventually, every attempt to reach out to her came to a complete stop once I moved on with my personal life.

 When I finally looked up, I noticed during the time frame of our (my daughter's father and I) dysfunctional relationship I was completely isolated from family and friends. The comfort of my sister moving in with me eased the blow of being alone and blocked any chance of me ever going backward and returning to the abuse. The man who became my husband, let's call him John, who was mentioned earlier in my baseline health as the young boy that I met when I was 13 years old in our local neighborhood recreation center happened to leave our neighborhood unbeknown to me. It wasn't until he returned home after joining the military that we ran into each other at a local club. We both were in there on Christmas with fake I.D's as we were both under the age of 21. It didn't take long for us to reacquaint but not long before we were comfortable talking. The club went up in an uproar as someone pulled out a gun and started shooting inside the club. People were running everywhere, jumping over the DJ booth, exiting out of non-exit doors, and literally running for our lives. I found myself in the parking lot with John and we ended the night going out to eat with friends and talking until the sun came up. Before the night ended, we exchanged numbers so that we could stay in touch. We revisited the idea of being more than just friends. I had already had a daughter that was a year old and he had a child who was three years old. I always wanted a big family of at least six children because I never had any siblings under the same roof. I didn't want my children to grow up alone, but more importantly, I wanted to create something I never had. I resented the fact that my mother ended up walking out and leaving my little brother in the county hospital after she gave birth to him in July 1988. She never took the responsibility of having another child and whoever the father seemed to not even be concerned. Not sure if that's the reason I found myself so passionate about being a mother. Yet, I still don't remember crying about that.

We began to talk regularly and we soon found ourselves engulfed in this long-distance relationship. Although he was not stationed locally, he would find his way down to Las Vegas for permitted and non-permitted visitations. It was not long before we found ourselves becoming a little more intimate during visitations. I became pregnant with my second child at the age of 21. Abstinence is the best way to avoid unwanted pregnancies; however, the thought of that was so far from my goals at that time. I remember telling him while he was back at his barrack. After hearing the fair but yet disrespectful question if I was sure that it was his child, I answered with an offended "yes." As the days went by, I can tell he was struggling with the fact of having to tell his mother because he actually had the balls to admit saying those exact words. He felt like he could not tell his mother that he had another child on the way and it became so overbearing to him that he had the nerves to ask me to have an abortion. I remember something rose inside of me and I told him with a bold voice that I would never consider having an abortion and with or without him I was going to have this baby. I laid down now I had to be responsible for my actions. It didn't take him long to realize the sincerity and truth in my voice and he decided to walk with me. I was so glad he did.

Finally, our son was born on the day that he was deployed. My aunt and sister were the only ones present during this time. It was bizarre because by the time the end of the day settled he called the hospital and found the both of us.

After my beautiful son was born I started having a reality check. Not only was I a mother of one baby but it was now two mouths to feed. At this time I was working at the medical clinic owned by an African American doctor whose sister-in-law was the office manager. She is a woman of power, grace, and honor. She carried herself like a boss chick but with a level of class that I never recognized growing up in the hood. She was also the president of a very prestigious organization called the Southern Nevada Black Nurses Association (SNBNA). She took a liking to me and an interest in my future. She began to invite me to meetings and with the help of her and the rest of the SNBNA members, I was well on my way to a bright future. I re-enrolled into college to complete what I had initially started which was nursing. Around the return to my commitment of education, my mother was diagnosed with HIV. I felt angry with this announcement for a few reasons. I immediately connected it to prostitution, it added to the embarrassment that I harbored after finally accepting my mixed race, now an embarrassing disease that has no cure, and even though we barely had a relationship I would have to be extremely cautious in her presence. Walking around on eggshells and in fear of everything around us. How inconvenient I selfishly thought. HIV can only be transmitted by saliva or blood usually by way of sex or drug use. It is true, I remained extremely cautious and it is still weird that I can't sit on my own mother's commode, I won't use her utensils or cups in fear of transmission and vice versa when I'd invite her to my home. Even though I was angry, I still don't remember crying. She has lived a healthy life for over 20 years without complications and she is still living at the age of 73. That's nothing but the grace of God.

    I will admit, furthering my education was difficult and I did do it stepping stones with earning my decree as LPN (Licensed Practical Nurse) at first, but then eventually, accomplishing what I thought was absolutely impossible which was my RN (Registered Nurse) degree. It did not

Transforming Into Disasters Worst Enemy

happen overnight but after a duration of 7 years, it was done. In the midst of those 7 years, I was blessed enough to utilize Section 8 housing as a crutch, medicaid health services, John and I were married, had a third child, going to school full time, taught praise dance at my church, and still maintained a full-time job. No matter how heavy the load my resilient spirit never gave up. Although returning and completing this degree meant that I finally had an opportunity to provide for my children a life that I never had, I failed to realize that it didn't happen without a cost. I do regret the time necessary that I had to sacrifice away from my children and husband to complete this task but didn't bother to ask if and did it affect them in any way. I know now as I'm analyzing my life this had to, even if subconsciously, affect them in some way. However, neither did I hear any complaints, especially after everyone was able to reap off the seed that I had sown. All so much that I even was promoted unknowingly by the man of the house to carry the family on my back via finances. As I remained an open book about finances, my friends, and all endeavors, I did not get that back in return. There were so many secrets between us as a couple such as but not limited to locked passcode phones, pay stubs were non-existing, he had friends I never met or knew where they lived yet he spent his weekend nights away with them. It's sad to say but I can now admit that we were still strangers after 17 years of marriage.

    The benefit of completing this degree did allow us to provide a life for our family that most of the people that came from our hood could yet experience. We became the model family for many couples that were in our circle. With all this growth I never lost my passion for my first love who is Jesus Christ. I would read my bible, bring the family together to pray, teach the children about God and we would attend church on Sundays. My husband was not all that interested in attending church as often as we did but would show up 1-2 Sundays out of the month. We had regular growing pains of a young marriage. You know a lot of shedding of oneself to ultimately become one. We had some favorable and unfavorable moments. I would admit that the majority of our marriage I choose not to deal with certain things in an attempt to keep peace between the two of us. In a nutshell, I was able to return to the unhealthy coping skills of my past of internalizing my feelings and walk around numb. Divorce had never been an option as I believed that Jesus Christ Himself honored marriages. Matter of fact, people would come to me for counsel when they would consider divorce and I would always push them in the direction of reconciliation, forgiveness, and counseling.

Transforming Into Disasters Worst Enemy

Remaining busy with the day to day life responsibilities of working, cooking, cleaning, wifely duties, and motherhood, I never recognized the underlying torture and adaptation that lay prominent in my children and myself. Life became a routine and I will admit that I was just existing and not actually living. I just knew how to make it work and in my selfishness pushed towards what it was supposed to look like in my head. I desired to be a family so bad that I was willing to sacrifice who I was in order to have it. I would see families at the church come in together with the man of the house present and active in the church. I began to yearn for my family to look like that. Now I began to harbor disappointment as I did not want to force a fake relationship in my home. The closer my relationship grew with the Lord the more I desired that my family would be saved. I couldn't understand why everyone did not want this relationship with the Lord as deep as I did. I started seeing a split between the girls and boys. The girls would get up, go to church with very little resistance, and be involved with the activities of the church like me. On the other hand, my boys would complain and ask if they could just stay home with dad. I learned when the mother is the only one saved 50-70% of the time the children would be saved but when the father is saved 100% of the time the children would be saved. Men don't realize the unspoken influence they have in a family. Especially those who are involved and are not just a present body in the home. Just like my uncle, I conformed to this same type of man with similar characteristics. I became content with him just coming home every night even if it was at 3:30 or 4:00 in the morning. After tireless arguments and pleads for change, I gave in because I believed that permitting this to continue was one of those give or take things that made a marriage work. Honestly, I hated when the weekend would come, knowing I could do nothing about it except suck it up and endure until the time went by. I would have my outburst from time to time but ultimately, his giving in was only to shut me up and I'd rather he leave instead of sitting in the home with a sour lemon face, non approaching attitude, and bad aura in my opinion.

    Living in a state of existence is completely unhealthy emotionally, mentally, and especially spiritually. Was I so caught up in trying to look normal that I was willing to sacrifice my happiness? As much as I despised being a people pleaser in the world, I became one in the home. There is no book other than the bible that can teach us how to parent or be wives or husbands. The Holy Spirit is a teacher and I know I ignored his soft, subtle but convicting voice over a great deal of my marriage and I know God was tired of it. Here I am with the family that I always wanted; 2 boys and 2 girls, a dog, a man, a home, a car, and a career. What more could I ask for? But there was still something missing. I missed my daddy, and the older I got the more I wanted him in my life. I would cry from time to time as I would imagine how my children would have responded to what I called a normal grandparent. Would he be proud of me, his adult daughter, and who I became? My uncle was in my life and for the time he was able to be a grandparent to my children was greatly appreciated. But that wasn't the only place I had a hole. Who was I really? Why was I created and what am I supposed to be doing? My life had become a mirage of my own imagination which left me susceptible as an open target to the death of my destiny.

    Now don't get me wrong, our marriage was not all bad. There was laughter in the house. Times of joy, communication, and expressions of gratitude. One of my favorites was going to the children's football, baseball, basketball games, or gymnastic/cheer performances together. Besides, we were friends first. I loved having a family so I expressed my love by trying to maintain a stable, nurturing, and peaceful environment. I kept the house clean, cooked every day, and talked to my children and husband about their day. Not realizing that I was probably more in love with the idea of looking like the perfect family I never had than actually having it and working on the deep issues of having a healthy family. I tried to arrange dinner at our six-chair table as often as possible through all the hustle, bustle, and various extracurricular activity schedules.

Theresa Padgett

We were totally consumed in our children's lives; however, we did find time to have date night from time to time. I have to admit the counselor asked me, what is that I like to do and I was at a loss for words. I never invested in myself to actually do something for me, to get my hair/nails done, engage in a hobby, or even have any alone time. Everything I did was for other people to be happy so I found a way to meet their needs in exchange for myself. Sounds like a typical co-dependent to me. I have to give my ex-spouse grace in knowing that he may have been doing the best he could have done as a husband and father as well. If we are not careful we can become a product of our environment. I am a woman who truly believes in the word of God. I had no problem submitting and allowing the man to be the head. I believe a man's home is his castle and was adamant about creating an oasis of harmony. Besides, a man, especially a black man goes through enough ridicule, strife, and stereotyping in the world. The world is already heavy on their shoulders and they have to work even harder to succeed. According to statistics, a black man from the hood should either be dead or in the penitentiary by the age of 25. Being that we were both from the same cloth, coming up on the westside of Las Vegas we vowed to present a better life to our children. We moved to a good neighborhood and gave them everything they ever wanted. We taught them principles about earning money; however, we still provided

Transforming Into Disasters Worst Enemy

more than what they needed. Depending on which child it was, they would soon feel as if they deserved the way of life they had. Their lights or gas was never off, they had a refrigerator full of food, they always had clean clothes, stayed warm or cool in weather, and named brand shoes. It became a routine that my ex-spouse would, in my opinion, replace the need of him just spending quality time with them with expensive shoes and games. I longed for him to just pull the boys aside and show them how to fix a car, take them to a movie, or out to eat. In the same lane, I wanted to hear him encourage the girls and tell them how beautiful and intelligent they were so no other man would be the first to tell them. I even went as far as buying a purity ring for my youngest daughter for Christmas and addressing it from her dad in hopes that she would take the sentimental gesture as a promise to him to remain pure. I would also receive lavish gifts for the holiday of items like designer purses and expensive perfumes that I knew we could not afford but I never questioned where the money came from. I made more money than him and I never made him feel like he was less than a man. I refused to allow him to feel insecure or unworthy in his own home. Unfortunately, even at the cost of mine and my children's emotional and mental health. Believing that certain extremes were taken because I did not know how to raise men so I turned a blind eye or a deaf ear to things until they got out of control with my older son. I would jump in when I felt like it was enough and just cease the noise. The fear and tension in the home when it was time for discipline almost made me feel as if I was the one being punished. I'm not perfect either, in my impatience and quick temper I did a great deal of yelling and screaming at the children. Making a whole bunch of noise and never saying anything. I realize that only made me feel better as it did my aunt and older cousin when they did it to me and wasn't adequate parenting. Naturally, it is only right that I take some responsibility for the damage that my children experienced.

      One thing I knew for sure was whenever I came in the presence of the Lord I never wanted to leave. Any time I could steal away to read or worship my love for the Most High God grew deeper and deeper. I would pour into the family what I had learned, pull everyone together to pray, and even have bible study with the children. Although, we would all come together as I prayed, over time I became content that my other half and I did not study together. I grew to accept the lack of spiritual growth in our relationship by applying excuses and finding scriptures that would warrant my silence. You can't make nobody do nothing and who am I to judge? Who knows maybe he would eventually transform into the man that God wanted him to be on HIS time, not mine then eventually my

Transforming Into Disasters Worst Enemy

patience would soon pay off. Or was it the man that I wanted him to be?

I started teaching praise dance and mime ministry in 2003 without ever seeing anyone do it. It was offered to me and I gladly accepted it as dance was a gift the Lord had given to me and to use it for His glory was undeniably an opportunity that I could not refuse. As the Holy Spirit taught me the art of worship, prophetic, praise, liturgical, and mime dance it became embedded in my DNA. I taught the art of dance and the principle of preaching the gospel through movement with not only physical usage of our limbs but total mind, body, and spirit. It was important that my students understood no matter how old they were that this was not a performance but ministry. The Lord would use me to extend my gift to other ministries outside of my church and ultimately the community. The Holy Spirit charged me with the task of creating, initiating, and executing a Performance Arts Workshop called Rise Up and Praise Him. The workshop as the Holy Spirit gave to me was targeted towards children as small as 7 years old all the way up to adults of all ages. The final piece was to take it outside the walls of the church and extend it to the community. My task was to find a theater in the community that would welcome the final showcase on their stage avoiding the traditional use of a church building and its audience. The first year was absolutely scary, mainly due to the fear of the unknown but the Lord did not leave me by myself. I had help through my aunt who allowed me to be a part of her non-profit organization and its connections in the westside community, a host of talented holy ghost-filled volunteers as teachers, administrators, and supporters. It wasn't just my church that was involved but so many different ministries that came together and executed perfection. It was a success and we are now as of 2021 working on our 4th Annual Rise Up and Praise Him Workshop. I foresee it growing bigger and more profound so that the voice of Rise Up will be heard across the nations and that everyone touched by this experience will never be the same.

    During the time I was dancing and attending church, people would tell me that dance was not all that the Lord had for me. Others would see in me things that I felt but did not believe about myself. I never felt ready but it wasn't long before my Pastor at the time would have put me up in front of the congregation to give the word. It was a humbling experience as when someone actually believes in you and trusts you enough with the flock that the Lord has assigned to them they have got to be sure. I remember watching other women of all ages confidently stand before the people and would always wonder how they got there? I never counted the cost, as in my journey, I was well on my way to be greater than I could ever imagine. Over the marriage, I remained conscious of my position as a wife avoiding the full dive into ministry. As he had made it clear that this was my thing and his weekend endeavors was his thing and too much of anything was not good for the relationship. He would give examples of wives who would go to church Sunday-Sunday and never tend to the family. I wasn't dumb, I knew that he didn't want me involved in church so much. I would skip bible study weeks, teach praise dance once a week for two hours unless we had an event to prepare for which my girls were with me on those days and I would avoid second services within the week or on Sunday unless we had to minister in dance all to maintain a balance. Yes, I would invite him but he wouldn't come. The Lord would not stop calling me to the works of ministry. No matter how often I would pull back the invites, to speak and minister in dance would not stop flowing. My life became content and I figured I had the balance all figured out. It wasn't until the Lord Himself allowed me to be uncomfortable as the very foundation that I built began to destroy. It was like a rug was pulled from underneath my entire life and everything that I thought I knew had fallen. In May of 2018, the first change that occurred was when the church home that I was so comfortable being a part of for 20 years of my life was about to come to an abrupt separation. It was time to move and it wasn't so much of what I wanted but it was because of who God was calling me to be. The Lord told me that I was loyal to man and not to HIM. My entire identity was wrapped up in my faithfulness to the children that I was teaching and the people I served under but not necessarily adhering to the voice of the Holy Spirit. This was true because I was committed and we had all become like family. I began to cry when I realized that the Lord was pushing me out of the nest. As it had been tugging for a long time but unfortunately I waited for a push of a disagreement to be the fuel that I needed to put myself first. It's a sad trait that I harbor because I will fight for everybody else but when it comes to me fighting for myself but somebody would have to make me angry enough then you better watch out. After a time, my Pastor and I did reconcile but that did not negate the fact that I had to remain obedient to the Lord. This pain was similar to the time when my husband at the time suggested that I was teaching and praise dancing too much and to consider stopping. I don't even remember crying in the flesh because before the words computed in my mind my very spirit began to weep. I cried from a place that I could never touch and the tears were so real. Needless to say, I boldly confess that I would not stop because this is what God wanted me to do. That was the one thing that I was not willing to relinquish.

    October 2018 turned into the beginning of a slow, torturous, overwhelming experience.

Transforming Into Disasters Worst Enemy

I was invited to a 2-day women's retreat in a deserted area about an hour and a half away from the Las Vegas area. I asked my ex husband if he was ok with me going and although I felt guilty leaving everyone, I still pushed through. I left everyone except my baby girl who joined me. When we got there we noticed that it was a dry, desolate place. You can tell there was once life, rivers, lakes, and trees there but now there were dry lake beds, dried out river trails, bent over, broken and dead trees everywhere. I thought to myself, did the coordinator really check this place out before we got here. Then she had the audacity to ask me to speak? Here's what I see now, I went expecting to be poured into but the Lord allowed me during my studies to be filled so I may pour into others. The Lord was preparing me for today. He gave me the Ezekiel 37 and as I was telling these women in this dry, desolate place to prophesy to their dry bones the Lord was preparing me in the desert as I was about to encounter some dead things that were about to rock my world. As we were sitting in the little church on the retreat property, our coordinator encouraged us to just sit, be still and hear from God. As I sat beside an open view window listening to the worship music in my view was the dry lake bed. I began to focus on worshiping the Lord so I closed my eyes and began to pray. Then I sat in silence and the Lord showed me a vision of myself in the dark with my arms extended from my body in worship and my head looking up towards the heavens. Suddenly, the sky opened and it began to rain bright blue fire directly into my chest. I could actually feel it as I sat in the natural. Then the rain began to flicker like an old light bulb going out. "No, no, Lord!" I said under my breath and I stood up in the natural, extended my arms in worship with my head lifted towards heaven. As I closed my eyes I began to see the heavens open up again and the blue fire began to pour into my chest again. Then not long after, it began to flicker again. I asked the Lord "What's wrong?" and He clearly said to me, "I cannot elevate you because you keep allowing distractions to get in the way." I left feeling empty, confused yet with a glimpse of expectation because I knew that the Lord wanted to do something in my life.

    After getting home from the retreat, I ran to my husband at the time telling him everything that I learned. I expressed how excited I was to learn that retreat meant to pull back in the war so one can be revived. How we can relate that to our walk in life. The importance of restoration and ironically we discussed that you can choose your sin but you cannot choose your consequences. You will get that later. Somewhere in my retreat notes, I found "If you're gonna reign with me, you must also suffer with me." Wow, why is this literally just now making sense to me in my current situation? God is so amazing. He truly equips His people for warfare. As I was talking I literally saw him staring right through me not connecting. Don't toss your pearls to pigs as scripture says. So, I ceased speaking and let him go on about his day. He was headed out somewhere and told me he would be right back. I was so excited about my day that I could not find anything to really do except sit on the bed and just enjoy the thoughts of the trip in my mind. As I sat on the edge of the bed I looked over to my left and saw a backpack on the side of the side table next to the bed. The Lord told me to unzip the zipper. I went to unzip the big zipper and the second I touched it the Lord said, "No, not that one, the little one." I then went to the litter zipper and opened the backpack. There was a small, silver phone present. I took the phone 'cause you all know my woman's intuition kicked in at that time and I needed no further instructions. The phone was unlocked…brilliant…and as I began to go through text messages, pictures and call logs my heart sunk deeper and deeper into my stomach. As I screamed "NO" from the top of my lungs it was a piercing sound that came from a place of betrayal and anguish. I know my children never heard that sound come from my bedroom before. I quickly wiped my face, took pictures of the screens on my phone, politely placed the phone in its rightful place then took off in my vehicle. I had nowhere to go as I drove aimlessly around the valley. I was too embarrassed to go into my friend's house after I pulled up, so I drove off again. My sister was on the phone trying to console me and begging me to just get off of the road. I was so angry and had already started preparing the way out. I literally started talking about splitting up debt, moving out, and how we were going to handle the current bills. I was over it and there was no talking me down. Finally, my sister convinced me to stop by one of my other friend's houses and I sat with her for about two hours before I came home. I showed her pictures, cried, and talked myself into accepting that I was going to make it and I could make it through divorce. By that time he had already returned home, and heard about me leaving and crying. He started calling and texting me but I ignored it. Finally, came the moment of truth. Was I going to fold and go against everything I said I was going to do? Was he going to lie or was it going to be all a big misunderstanding? He was lying nonchalantly in the bed with his legs crossed almost positioned prematurely like he did nothing wrong. I asked him, "Are you cheating on me?" He denied it of course, and as I began to send pictures to his phone of conversations and pictures that he had and took with this woman on his secret phone. I then posed the question again and he was unable to deny the truth any longer. He began to plead and cry about it not being my fault and how sorry he was. I was completely numb. All of my emotions were out of the window and I was in a full drive of survival mode. It was time to discuss the splitting of the debt, house, and how we were going to move forward with divorce and the new life for our children. I proceeded to tell him to let this woman wash his dirty draws, to clean his home, and cook for him. I reaffirmed my promise that if he ever cheated on me that I would leave because I could never come back from that. I meant it. This was a choice that he made knowing that. Although I had no clue of the journey that lay before me I was prepared to step out on faith. That day my marriage died and it was time to prepare the funeral. This is my story and I am now at a point where it is no longer embarrassing to talk about.

    The entire night was full of uncomfortable episodes of him pleading, explanations, accusations, and guilt trips. It's sad to say but I don't remember crying in front of him yet I still had sympathy. I was mad at myself because I cared about him being in a state of desperation, pain, and guilt. The one time I could smash up his car, break his laptop, smack him in the face I couldn't ignore my feelings for him or my morals. The most I did was toss the secret phone over the balcony. I didn't want him to be at my mercy but rather to accept the repercussions he created like a man and walk away. I maintained a hard, stubborn but yet confident demeanor. My mind was made up. There was no turning back from my decision.

    The next morning as I lay in the bed with my son, he asked me to return to bed but I declined. He left and then the unexpected occurred. I received a phone call about 30 minutes after he left and he, on the other end, was in a voice that I never heard out of the thirty-plus years of me knowing him. Without revealing too much the level of intensity and fear is unexplainable but I feared his life was in danger. How selfish! I thought to myself. How could you put us through more torment? After a short period of riding this emotional rollercoaster, he was convinced to return to the house. Immediately that day we both went to counseling. At that point, I chose to stay and work it out and without ever admitting the truth. Oddly, I didn't want him to be hurt nor did I want my children hurt. But then again, to be real with myself, I couldn't let go of the idea of having a family. I was willing to suck it up and at least try to get past the infidelity. Who knows, it may work. My marriage is not the only marriage that suffered infidelity. There are many women who remained with their unfaithful spouses. Why couldn't I do the same? I began to convince myself that maybe the Lord would even use our testimony to help heal other marriages. All I knew was that I was buried under all of this rubble. My little fairy tale world of stability, love, and trust came to an abrupt halt as everything that I thought we were came crumbling down on top of me. The shakiness and uncertainty of our surrounding walls brought embarrassment and shame. The heaviness from the debris, steel, and ashes made it hard to breathe. Anxiety began to develop from feeling as if I was stuck and had no choice in my decision. There were no oxygen masks on site yet if I would just slow down my breathing and concentrate on expanding my lungs, breathing in and out I could remain calm. Depression started setting in as I lost hope in ever recovering from such a traumatic event. Would I ever get out of this place alive? It was time to tap into survival mode and it was evident that although it was a devastating, destructive disaster I did not suffer a fatal blow. I was still alive. Now the question is did I have enough or any of the essential elements to survive? Air, Water, and Temperature? Was my baseline health strong enough to take this blow and recover? We will find out as we walk this journey. Just as my mother went back to what she knew when devastation hit her with the loss of my father. I too turned to the only thing that I knew. Except it was not prostitution. I began a battle of seeking the Lord through the distraction of finding comfort, affirmation and a sense of belonging in others. We are troubled on every side, yet not distressed; we are perplexed, but not in despair; Persecuted, but not forsaken; cast down, but not destroyed; 2Cor 4-8, 9 KJV

Chapter 3
Air (Mind)

One of the three necessities of survival underneath the rubble after any disaster is the access to uninterrupted oxygen. Oxygen is all around us in the air that we breathe. Imagine being in a tight confined space where getting enough oxygen in your lungs becomes a task, a fight, or a struggle. That's how I felt after learning about the infidelity that took place in my marriage. That's right, after a long 17 years of marriage, my husband cheated on me. This was the earthquake that initiated the destruction that left me beneath the rubble, dark, alone, and afraid. Gut punched, devastated, and tormented by the reality that took place; unable to catch my next breath as it was all so unexpected that the ability to take it all in was so foreign that I could not comprehend the state I was in. Constantly, assuring people that I was fine only became a lie that I myself even believed.

Transforming Into Disasters Worst Enemy

Oxygen is so important that it will lead to death if we are deprived of it for only a short time and we tend to take it for granted that we have access to it. The reality is that we unconsciously live day to day without even thinking about the number of breaths we were graced with to continue to live. Just as we live day to day without being conscious of our breaths I found myself living day to day without being conscious of the environment that I lived in because I thought I was living a "Huxtable Family" lifestyle. For those who are not aware of the Huxtable family, it was a sitcom in the '80s and '90s that represented an upper-class black family who hashed out many common family issues with example-like lessons infused with comedy. Many of us watched from our poverty-stricken environments yet were drawn to the site of the family structure having a father that was active and present, especially those of us whose families did not look like theirs. Our family, friends, and peers marked my life as the family to mimic during this time. A beautiful home, careers, success, nice cars, a dog, a mother, a father, and lovely children. Loved ones actually admitted that their strength to leap forward into marriage was encouraged by our family. The truth was we were existing day to day but not actually living. Others who have to use assistance to regulate their breathing with personal oxygen machines, svn treatments or inhalers, and worse case scenario respirators are more conscious of the need to breathe because at any moment without these aspirates death is definite. It wasn't until my breathing was breached that the scales were removed from my eyes. Now I need an aspirates and what was I going to reach for? 7minutes of no oxygen to the brain for a victim leads to brain death. I was unable to think clearly or logically interpret even where I stood in all of this chaos. The air that I needed was equivalent to my mind but instead I reached out to other people.

  After spending several months in brokenness it began to lead me into depression. I couldn't let go of the image of perfection, love, and a family. This destruction revealed some hurtful things about the people that I held dear to me. Masks were removed and the truth of those I love has been exposed. I want to say, perhaps it's been there all along but I chose to turn a blind eye to reality. I even convinced myself that we were meeting the American family's expectations to live in peace and harmony therefore never confronting any real embedded issues. To live a safe, drama-free, family-orientated lifestyle, I avoided some needed conversations claiming it as submissiveness. That family-oriented lifestyle showed happy, in love parents that were present daily that spent every waking moment together without any complaints. That the children sincerely cared for one another, were goal-inspired, respected, and loved their parents to the fullest. Then to wrap it all up, the entire family was on one accord gratefully God-fearing and serving the Lord with our very lives. Where did I turn wrong? Who was I kidding? Were these just the images I made myself to believe? Did we really instill faith, obedience, and greatness in our children while the two of us were living two separate lives? I believe although we were different we simultaneously taught our children through different lessons. At which some were good, some were bad; however, accepting the fact neither of us is perfect unfolds the truth about grace and mercy. I'm more distraught about the fact that they had a choice because we were not on the same accord when it came to this Christian walk. Even worse that selfish spirit of lust and sexual immorality are both self-gratifying and will go beyond lengths to please those who harbor it….even at the cost of destroying a family. I felt isolated and suffered silently all while trying to hold all of whatever this was together for everyone but myself.

    The holiday season was coming up and I couldn't believe I'm still here. Still taking our yearly trips to see my sister in Sacramento for Thanksgiving,

Theresa Padgett

like nothing happened, smiling in our family faces, having family gatherings all the while hoping it would be over soon. This was definitely out of my character for I love family but it was too much pain to really trust that anything was real anymore. I asked him to change a few things that would possibly make our family better and mend the brokenness between the both of us. John wore those hats for about 2 months and he slowly returned to his normal self. I never made mention of it because I needed him to change because he wanted to change. Underneath this rubble began to get more and more uncomfortable and hard to camouflage. It was getting darker, heavier, and more confined. My desperate need to get air led me to the first tactic of this success story and that was consciousness. Yes, in order to breathe I needed to stop and seriously think. Consciousness is the awareness of one's own existence, sensations, thoughts, and surroundings. I had to be still and observe how my family was moving around me, what was reality, and most of all, who am I?

Oxygen fuels our cells and helps provide the basic building blocks that our bodies need to survive. Oxygen is also necessary for constructing replacement cells for our bodies. Every day about seven hundred billion cells in our bodies wear out and must be replaced. Without oxygen, our bodies cannot build these new cells. What was really happening? Was I so far underneath the rubble that I didn't trust that God would be able to rebuild what I had lost? I failed to equate God to the air that I breathed but the longer I sat underneath the rubble the more conscious I was. Living in disbelief I became numb and unresponsive to the situation. At counseling, one day in December, we discussed some things that I was unable to really wrap my mind around. How do one display compassion to someone who claims their hurt is stemming from the hurt they caused you? At this point, not hurting enough. I know Christ was compassionate and He's a perfect example but I couldn't get my heart and mind to agree. Here I am, completely torn with the decision that so often ran across my mind. Do I stay or go? In the far distance, I see complete forgiveness and healing. I'd be able to trust him again and God would show me how to love from a totally different place. A better, rejuvenated, bent but not broken type of relationship. On the other hand, I envisioned myself starting over without the guilt of choosing me for once. Seeing and daring to begin a new life. Let's be real, with all the selfishness that I endured, the lack of emotional support, and narcissistic behavior I thought this was a part of marriage. To endure the flaws, imperfections, and harboring my anger was submissiveness? I did realize as time went on there was a 12-year-old boy still in there that we never wanted to disrupt. Wondering if this is what God wants for me. He did however bring it to my attention. I had no clue on which way to go but what I did know was that I did love my husband and so desperately wished it never happened. I was so angry, disappointed, bitter, furious, ashamed, broken, afraid, insecure, and doubtful. What if he was waiting until the smoke cleared to pick up to repeat his actions? This is what children go through not grown folks after 4 children and 17 years of marriage. At least if there was a reason I could work on some things but I'm being told "It's not you, it's me." If it's you don't take my heart along for the ride. Verbalizing the constant pain from the wound of betrayal our counselor had to reiterate the fact that this trauma was equal to PTSD and trust is the first to go and the last to come back. He encouraged us to study the fruits of the Spirit. My bible tells me that grapes are not gathered from thorn bushes nor figs from thistles and that you will know them by their fruits. Consciously thinking, what type of fruit did I begin to bear underneath this rubble?

  The human eye is in critical need of oxygen to function properly. Oddly enough, the eye receives oxygen in a manner that is unique from the rest of the body. Few blood vessels travel to the eye, so our eyes absorb much of the oxygen they need directly through the cornea. The cornea is built in such a way to diffuse oxygen directly into the body from the air. This leads me to believe that not only did the things I need have direct access to me but the things I didn't need also have direct access to me. I've always been told that the eye is the window to the soul simply meaning you can understand a person by looking into their eyes. I was walking around with a great deal of hurt and although I wasn't gripping or complaining people would always ask questions about my well-being. Hiding the fact that I was cheated on and was contemplating divorce was the only way I felt survival could occur. I was so ashamed and didn't want anybody to know.Unfortunately, there were people who noticed and as this story unfolds you will understand how allowing people in during your most vulnerable time can do more harm than good. All in all, I began to look in the mirror and ask myself who am I really? Was I a failure, a quitter, or a runner because I wanted out? Was I trying to survive or be victorious?

It is through the human body's respiratory system that the cells of the human body receive the oxygen that they need to properly function. The entry "gates" of the respiratory system are the mouth and nose. This is where the air comes into the human body and this air is then directed toward and down the trachea into the lungs. Where am I right now? The entry gates to my life were fully exposed and unsecured. I had so many thoughts going through my head that the only way to slow them down was to not deal with them. Elisabeith Kubler-Ross wrote a book in 1969 named "5 Stages of Grief." It is only natural that whenever a human suffers a loss whether it is a job, marriage, a pet, finances, or death in a family one would go through the process of grieving. These stages are denial, anger, bargaining, depression, and finally acceptance. No one has a time limit on how long they will spend in each stage and if they would ever reach acceptance. This is something important to discuss with your partner if you are working through your marriage after such a disaster. Sometimes the choice is to work it out but these phases are still the human's normal response to the loss of trust. If they are not willing to roll up their pants legs and get in the mud to be there with you through the phases although they may feel you are overstaying perhaps they are not for you. We all have something we are struggling with and I believe the idea of a perfect person is an example of how I was living, an overstayed, unhealthy fairytale. I found myself in a short period of denial, back and forth with anger, never experiencing bargaining but spending an overdue amount of time in depression. I was mourning my marriage and living in the house was like attending a live funeral. No changes were made on his end and I found myself snapping and apologizing often because I never was given the space to begin the healing process. Back and forth fighting myself internally and seeking an answer from God I was not sure on what to do.

    I long to be free…

    Free from the torment of these thoughts in my head

    These thoughts that keep telling me that my marriage is dead.

    What's the use of trying?

    Your love will end up drying.

    At this point, you barely have a pulse, the beat is way too faint.

    You keep trying to draw a picture of trust while using a dry can of paint.

    I long to be free…

    And just love him with all of me. In the end, it would all be a waste…

    If he turns around and just spits in my face.

    What if he's addicted to being disloyal?

    When the smoke clears, my heart will spoil.

    What happens when he gets tempted again?

Theresa Padgett

Will he f*** then look into my face and grin...again?

I'm pissing myself off, I just can't stop thinking about it.

You dare toss 17 years of my love in the toilet like s**t?

This b**** face keep occupying space in my brain,

I think I'm over it but then it happens all over again.

How selfish is a man who'd risk it all just to cum

This s*** got me wishing my emotions were numb...

I long to be free...

Am I in bondage and the warden is...me?

Can I let myself go?

Forsake all that I know?

I question, are we meant to be together?

Got what it takes to move past this weather?

The storm is so strong, I can barely see

But to find out the one who holds the umbrella is me.

This realization is too much to handle

Making this decision is truly a gamble

Transforming Into Disasters Worst Enemy

He's giving up trying, seems he's just waiting to see which route I'm traveling

Not understanding, he needs to pursue me harder to keep me from unraveling...

Dude, don't you get it? You are not the victim.

Yes, you got feelings but YOU put us "in" them.

Love me harder even if I push back

How bad do you want our love back on track

I long to be free...

To trust without a wall in front of me

Unlike Trump, who built it to keep the immigrants away

I built it then allowed these foreigners to stay...

I'm going through like a see-saw on a playground

My emotions are in a whirlwind, tossing me all around

This is traumatic, I long to be free...

What is the antidote and how much is the fee?

Gotta see what the end is going to bring,

Halfway in with my heart on my wings

Feeling unprotected, insecure, and unsafe

Like a tsunami hit and washed my love away...

Is it recoverable, will it be revived back again?

To love him freely even in the wind?

Theresa Padgett

Damn, this here is not fair, I don't deserve it.

Got caught off guard with my hands in my pockets…

I long to be free….

And I mean free indeed

Am I searching for the wrong thing? Should I just let it be?

Keep thinking about him but what about me?

It's time to make changes and right now I see very few…

Am I the key to his change? Should we split and start life anew?

I'm too embarrassed to talk to women with wisdom,

So, I tend to harbor these thoughts, cry internally so I don't look dumb…

I long to be free   I long to be free…

Chapter 4
Temperature (Body)

Now that I regained my consciousness I was able to see this situation and those around me for what and who they really were. The old and even the new people that came in and gained my trust. I started behaving in a way that was contradicting to my character. It's amazing how we can create a whole facade in our minds and actually make ourselves believe it. Even to the point of believing what I felt was real and even worse how I made everyone else feel as I tried to fit them into my make-believe world. Yes, not only was I able to see everyone else during this destruction the Lord was showing me myself. I thought I was a flawless mother and wife doing all the right things yet neglecting to ever have those conversations on what was real. These conversations could have initiated the much-needed growth, healing and areas of change in my life. Still trapped underneath the rubble I was now able to control my breathing. I was actually getting air but the enclosed space around me led me to believe that I was not getting enough oxygen almost as if I was suffocating. I was moved by what it looked like such as the darkness, large rocks, and added pieces of broken metal in my world. It was a horrendous mountain of destruction that appeared too heavy to move.

The air (mind) was in a safe zone but what about my temperature (body)? A maintained temperature is important in order to increase the chances of one to make it out alive. The average person has a baseline temperature between 98°F (37°C) and 100°F (37.8°C). Your body has some flexibility with temperature. However, there is a process called thermoregulation that occurs to allow your body to maintain its core internal temperature if you were ever to get off balance. Underneath this rubble, I began to experience both hyperthermia and hypothermia.

Hyperthermia is just a fancy word used to express that the core temperature of the body is too high. Even to go further is to define it as the body being at a dangerously high level that could be damaging if left untreated. During this phase, everything began to move so quickly. I began to stress at a level that I never felt before. Feeling as if my body remained in a continuous fight or flight mode.

Transforming Into Disasters Worst Enemy

Although I was careful not to have any outward expressions of trauma it was evident in the amount of weight I was losing. I quickly dropped from a size 9 pants to a size 6. I still had an appetite but was not eating enough or healthy. The children and I moved into a new home, however, my youngest son wanted to stay with his father. Completely uncertain about our future, I was left with the sureness that our new reality was forcing us to deal with it whether we were ready or not. I could not get the children in counseling quick enough. I was so busy juggling the changes, carrying on with day to day responsibilities, and trying to make sure everyone else was good, somehow I forgot about myself. Anxiety and depression snuck up on me suddenly and I would find myself crying out of nowhere. As you have read, my coping mechanisms were amazing, however, it did not make them healthy. I ignored, avoided, and became numb. I didn't turn to drugs or alcohol but I began to wrap myself up in a man prematurely and busy work in the church. This rubble is so heavy there's no way I'm going to make it. I began to doubt and even contemplate if I was taking this divorce too far. But as things began to unfold during the divorce process other things became exposed that only confirmed my decision was what was best and final. As the foundation was broken the ground in my vision began to teal like a roaring wave and all kinds of dirt, broken glass, trash began to appear. All these secrets were hidden and it was unbelievable what was exposed.

My body was the point of focus and in order to be safe, I had to get it out of harm's way. Being exposed to hyperthermia for long periods of time could be deadly. The body has several natural mechanisms internalized that will activate in an effort to cool itself down. We are all familiar that increased activity, sunshine, or exercise causes us to sweat. Yes, sweating cools your skin off as it evaporates. So, the shame of the loss of my family and the feelings of failure and defeat were only present to mold me. The sweat from all the stress was the good by-product of hyperthermia but the devil meant it for evil and to destroy me. Let me make it clear, the sweat and tears were there to cool my body off from the pain; therefore, what the pain that the devil meant for evil my God turned the byproduct of the pain around for good.

Vasodilation is another mechanism that cools the body off. The blood vessels under your skin get wider. This increases blood flow to your skin where it is cooler away from your warm inner body. This lets your body release heat through heat radiation. It

Transforming Into Disasters Worst Enemy

became necessary to release or suffocate. Dilation simply means to open up. Something I had been so unfamiliar with my entire life. Who would want to hear what I had to say, my opinions, my dreams, aspirations, or future endeavors? Who could I trust enough to really open up to? The Lord was tugging at me to draw nearer to Him. Come on, prayer is what I do, there's no way I needed to enhance my prayer life, I talked to Him daily. Boy, was I wrong! The Lord began to show me that although I pray I haven't truly opened up and emptied myself out before Him. More importantly, I wasn't listening. It's not the superficial act of prayer but, more importantly, the intimate dialogue and reverence of the Holy Spirit. God was calling me to deeper depths and higher heights in Him and there was an urgency for me to get there.

My daughter's counselor and others close to me began to point to the need for me to get therapy. No way, I got this! I've been surviving under the ashes and rubble this long without dying or giving up. My children need me and I can't slow down for me. As the days, weeks, months went on the pressure began to be evident. I figured I'd give a counselor a try. The combination of talking with the counselor and the Holy Spirit I began to learn things about myself that I wasn't proud of. Learning how to put myself in other people's shoes and, most importantly, to accept who God says that I am. It was like being introduced to a new person. I found myself going through periods of depression, anger, and denial all over again as I tried to process these realities. But as I mentioned before no one can tell you how long or even how many times you will encounter steps in the stages of grief. The heat was on and the more vulnerable I became to releasing control the more effective the healing process became. I did not release some areas without many lessons.

The complete opposite of hyperthermia is hypothermia. You guessed correctly, it means to have a core temperature below the regular baseline. It's ironic that remaining in either of these two states too long could be detrimental. Once again, we serve a God in His infinite power who has created the human body in such a way that no man on planet earth could have ever conjured it up or recreated its perfection in a lab.

The body's natural defense to hypothermia is vasoconstriction. This is better described as when the blood vessels under the skin get smaller which then increases the blood flow to the skin warming the body up. Let's be clear, there were never any moments of serenity as I toggled intensely between periods of overwhelming heat and treacherous coldness. The coldness were periods of loneliness, fear, and guilt.

Transforming Into Disasters Worst Enemy

Blaming myself for staying too long or even leaving at all. Blaming myself for all the pain my children endured. Blaming myself for being a coward, overlooking things, and choosing not to have a voice. Placing the idea of looking like a family and not being one at the expense of my personal growth or listening to God. Usually, when addicts go through detox they become sick, nauseous, diarrhea, and trembling. Uncontrolled trembling sounds uncomfortable but during hypothermia, the body's natural defense is to cause shivering of the muscles to produce heat. Okay, so was the sickness actually part of the healing process? Late nights of crying, screaming, and feelings of unworthiness alone in my room being fearful to return to the old way or move forward in a new normal? Nurturing bad coping mechanisms because I was too impatient to wait on God? Entertaining bad company that would ultimately corrupt my morals?

Since the Lord created the body to self-regulate by using what was already built in it now it was time for me to be like my Father. I had a great deal of anger, impatience, and frustration in this body. So the only logical thing to do was to use it as firepower. The real definition of firepower is the capacity to deliver effective fire on a target. To bring about it in a potent way which means to bring about a particular result. My aim was becoming precise during this period and the building of the firepower was becoming more intense. My temperament was changing rapidly and healing for my children and myself became the unwavering target. As I was treating a patient one Tuesday morning, he was listening to a song on his speakerphone. I couldn't help but to be intrigued by the words. Listening in detail I felt my heart expand with inspiration to keep fighting, my spirit was lifted in courage as I struggled to hold back any tears. I asked him the name and artist of the song."Blowback" is the name of this song. The song told a story about a woman who was considered to be poor, white trash who was determined to change. She packed up everything and left her past behind without fear as she had been there, done that, and tried it all. There was nothing there to hold her back any longer. It was the realization of her circumstances (consciousness) that allowed her to use what she experienced and who she was within as firepower. In order to do so, she needed to breathe in the blowback. Blowback is the process where gases expand or travel in the direction opposite especially through pressure or delayed combustion. Usually, the crowds of people disperse and run away from the presence of a blowback combustion, especially if it's too close. In contrast, this woman ran towards the blowback! Silently saying I am not afraid, tired of the combustion in my life and now I'm going to attack the very thing that kept me defeated. In my opinion, her destiny was on the other side of the combustion, and in order to get to it, there was no way over, underneath, or around it. Running through it was her only option even if she risked a few minor cuts, burns, or scraps. Fascinating enough the blowback is the result of an item combusting but if I charge forward I will run past not only the blowback but that which combusted, leaving it in the past and ultimately defeating it! Pastor Sarah Jakes said, "You cannot become who you are becoming and who you were at the same time."

But now, this is what the Lord says— he who created you, Jacob, he who formed you, Israel: "Do not fear, for I have redeemed you; I have summoned you by name; you are mine. When you pass through the waters, I will be with you; and when you pass through the rivers, they will not sweep over you. When you walk through the fire, you will not be burned; the flames will not set you ablaze." Isa 43:1-2

Chapter 5
Water (H2O)-(Spirit)

Water is the third and final essential item needed to live both under the rubble and in freedom. The water represents the Spirit. Air, temperature and water are all essential. It's imperative to understand that having one without the other will not save you. The revelation comes from understanding that some fights are won by the ability to come up with an unexpected yet deadly combo. Those one-hit punches, jabs, and uppercuts may work for a little while but they become ineffective. They result in getting blocked because after being in the fight for so many rounds the component can see them coming. This devil has studied my fighting technique for far too long and now through this tedious training period, the Lord is transforming me into disaster's worst enemy by reformatting my weapons. The Lord has downloaded some combos that are leaving my enemy shook, dizzy, and dazed. I'm training for an undeniable TKO and I'm not stopping until this fool is lying on his back. Air without water will still lead me to death from dehydration. Appropriate thermoregulation without air will still lead to suffocation. Air being the mind, temperature being the body and finally, I will explain how the water correlates to the Spirit.

The average adult is made up of 60% water. Water is essential to keeping your body functioning properly and feeling healthy. According to Mayo Clinic, nearly all of your body's major systems depend on water to function and survive. On average, a female needs 9 cups of water per day, and males need 13 cups per day. If a person is under rubble, is uninjured, has an air supply, and is in an adequate space the next priority is water. The average person can survive 3-7 days without it. Once again, the other factors we've discussed earlier ties in with how long a person may survive without water as related to baseline health, the temperature if it's causing them to sweat or if they are losing fluids secondary to vomiting or diarrhea can lead to a greater need to replenish the water supply quicker. Dehydration is very serious and can affect your heart and body temperature, cause fatigue and possibly result in death. So as we can see, all three affect one another. Likewise, to the mind, body, and spirit. One must be conscious, have firepower, and finally the pertinacity to walk out the fire pit like Shadrack, Meshack, and Abendigo, or better yet the lion's den like Daniel unharmed and free. To go even a little further, they all endured a place of uncomfortability and remained vulnerable to trust the Lord would bring them out.

Pertinacity is a quality of sticking with something, no matter what. It's a type of persistent determination that is unwavering and not easily destroyed. During this time, I noticed my water reservoir was full but not overflowing. Yes, that's right, I had just enough to survive but not able to affect those around me. I know what you're asking, "What's wrong with surviving?" Just surviving was causing me to live underneath the planned destiny that the Lord has for me. So you may be comfortable with just well enough but greater things my God said that I would be able to do! I began to notice that there were many obstacles I allowed to come in between me and my destiny. It became even worse as deception crept through the broken cracks of my healing process. Appearing only to finish me off and to leave me in an unrecoverable position. Believe it or not, a healthy stream will have a lot of obstacles in its channel such as rocks and fallen logs. What does that mean? Some of these will capture materials washing down the stream to form small debris dams that produce pools of water on their upside and spills of water as it passes over the debris. This spillage mixes bubbles of air into the water, increasing its oxygen content to the benefit of stream invertebrates and fish. Wow, although obstacles sound like a problem they still produce a needed source that is imperative to me making it out alive. Not only that, the overflow was able to benefit those around. My change produced change in others. My growth initiated growth in others. The oxygen that is produced as the water moves over the debris helps the stream move faster and with more force. How does the water even know to keep pushing or how to gauge its power to continue? Rocks in the stream channel produce riffles of shallow flow, which are the preferred habitat for some species. Christ is the rock! It's all connected in a way that not only will obstacles produce in me the pertinacity to keep going but will also produce out of me greatness if I tap into the rock. The rock which is in control of the movement of the river. In short, a healthy stream will not simply carry water downslope at high speeds, but promote a slow, meandering movement of water that rejuvenates it. It may look inefficient, but it will be a healthy ecosystem. The natural flow of water in any stream or river demonstrates a much-needed source to draw pertinacity and how to be conscious of the obstacles so they may be utilized as firepower.

What's important is to avoid being stagnant. I believe this is where I lived over the past 20 years of my life but you will see how the Lord began to reveal and bring me out. I won't sit here and claim regretting everything I encountered because I wouldn't be who I am today. Yes, it was all for the making and the building for HIS glory. If I could have been prepped for 2018 I would have worn a hard hat instead of a party hat on New Year's Eve. As mentioned earlier in this book, the comfortability that was on my job, church home, and family were quickly snatched from under me like a giant rug. I became stagnant in my growth in the Lord, my relationship in HIM, and more importantly, the ambition to reach higher heights. I cannot point the finger at anybody else but myself. Stagnant water no longer moves and it attracts bugs, bacteria, and viruses which if dwelling too long can cause sickness, disease, or even death. Now, this is where the revelation comes in. If water represents the spirit my comfortability was leading to the ultimate destruction and death of my spiritual life. I'm almost embarrassed to admit it but I was choosing my desires over the Lord's will for me. Aborting my destiny and willing to allow life to go by, eventually burying all these books, conferences, dance studios, new business endeavors, and abundance of life in the grave? The Lord has given me gifts beyond measure not for me but for His people. To be able to touch them through so many different avenues to cause change, encouragement and ultimately lead them to a better life through Christ Jesus. If you are reading this book you need to understand that I know now that my exodus was imperative to your exodus. Are you in bondage to anything? Are you stagnant? Have you built your own safe haven and only appear to the world that you have it all together? Don't get comfortable thinking that today is the best that God has for you. I want all that the Lord has for me. I don't want to wait until I die to enjoy a piece of heaven. I am the King's kid and through inheritance have been born to eat the best fruit, wear the best clothes and have the best health. Exodus simply means a mass departure of people. Everything that's attached to me shall also get free and be blessed more abundantly and likewise to you.

I was becoming a woman of fortitude. What's even more astounding is the realization that she was always there. After remaining in the home for an additional 12 months the Lord released me. All the confusion and indecisiveness began to melt away as the 8-month weights of depression were lifted. The Lord showed me that vision of the road splitting and it was evident. I could see clearly now, there was clarity and confidence. We were going in two different directions, as hurtful as it was to let go of everything I knew in this relationship and to move on. One thing for sure, I had no clue on what I was moving forward to do. I had to trust God and lean not on my own understanding. Although I was confident that God released me, I will admit I still was trying to do things my way. The road I began to tread on was leading me into unnecessary obstacles and chaos. I was making some bad choices and going down a road in desperation that could only offer additional rubble on top of the rubble I was already under. Like a wounded animal I did not use good judgement to shelter myself from vultures that actually feed on the weak, vulnerable and wounded. Like unlocked doors leave access to unwanted guests so does careless behavior leave unwelcome access for spiritual attacks.

On March 17, 2020, the entire country shut down because of the coronavirus. We were all placed under strict instruction to self-quarantine in our homes unless we worked in an essential field. My job was nursing, therefore, without a choice, I had to suit up in a mask and gloves and continue to work. The schools, churches, small businesses, parks, restaurants, movies,

Transforming Into Disasters Worst Enemy

hair salons/barber shops, and you name it, were shut down. Living in Las Vegas I never saw the strip empty and during this season there were absolutely no signs of life, lights, or action down there. Although I was still pulling 40 hours a week I couldn't help but encounter the same type of quarantine as everyone else. God's hand was all over this and what I began to realize was that the quarantine was necessary to abolish all unnecessary distractions so we as his people would draw near Him. It was a time to self-reflect, find ourselves, and build a closer relationship with yourselves, families and the Lord. A time to actually pour into our children, love our spouses if applicable, and do something we never had time for...communicate.

    I can say that this is where the lump sum of the healing process and transformation took place. I became a better mother during this season and was able to live more consciously for the destiny of my children. In the cocoon of life, I was transforming into a beautiful butterfly. Although I was becoming impatient as I was ready to fly I noticed how the Lord wouldn't allow the process to speed up. Just like a caterpillar who comes out of the cocoon too soon, it would die and the entire process would be a waste of time. I can even go a little further and say that even the time of the existence of the caterpillar was in vain because it never finished its purpose. The Lord even told me to stop saying that infidelity is the reason for my divorce. I'm thinking "Did you not see what I saw?" To go even further, I was told that it wasn't my fault nor was it my partner's fault. If I wanted to stay where would I start? How do you try to fix something and you have no starting point? Yet, I had no desire to fix it but the more I thought about the pain and anguish it caused my ex, my children, and myself the more I felt bad about my choice. Questioning God if I really made the right decision. No, it wasn't my ex-husband, the infidelity, or myself as to why the marriage could no longer exist. It was deeper than that. We wrestle not against flesh and blood but principalities. There is an enemy that wants to destroy us and by our choices assist it further along. Before you allude to the idea that the Lord destroyed our marriage I want to stop you there. That is not the case at all, as a matter of fact, the Lord gives us free will and allows us to choose. I did however put my relationship with the Lord on the back burner. Sacrificing what He wanted to do in my life, blocking my destiny, ignoring the fact that He chose me so I could not move how I wanted to move. The truth is that I was playing church and turned off the sound from heaven. I'm noticing now that the Lord has been talking to me for a long time but I choose to ignore him. Not taking the time to pray, listen, or even consult the Lord unless life was challenging. I will also admit to the fact that because the enemy is the author of confusion I thought I was justified by the scripture. I really believed that submission to your husband meant in regards to everything and home is your first ministry, therefore, everything and everybody else was obsolete even when it came to ministry outside of the home. Why, because the Lord honors the marriage. Although, my destiny was tugging at me to come higher and higher and I could feel the word like fire shut up in my bones. I was literally walking away from what I was created to do. I would turn down ministry engagements and feel convicted by the Holy Spirit but then again accept engagements and feel guilty. It was a need for balance but the scales were not even. We were unequally yoked. Truth is this walk wasn't as important to me 20 years ago as it is to me now but knowing your foundation is solid in Christ and you share the same morals is always a good sign that a relationship can survive the waves and growth spurts of life. Why? Because we both have a common denominator and place we can both go back to regroup. We used to yell "safe" when we would play hide and seek and make it to base. Your foundation should always represent a safe place in your marriage but it means nothing and will not stand if you build two separate foundations. Everything built on it eventually would cave in and crumble, the weight of the structure would be unbalanced and shaky. Not that he does not identify with being a Christian but this walk is more in-depth than what comes out of our mouths. That applies to me as well. I learned for myself that surrendering to God's will is visual and evident in continued growth and change. When our marriage ended and God showed me the vision of two roads separating from one solid track indicating that we were going in two separate directions I realized that I could no longer travel with him towards my destiny. See everybody can't go where you're going and the sooner you realize this is not your life but God's life the quicker you will accept the changes that take place.

  As time moved forward, I also was learning the true meaning of forgiveness. I thought forgiveness also was justified when you decide to stop dealing with someone. You know the saying, I forgive him/her but I'm not dealing with them anymore. I forgave a lot of people like that. Being that I and this man have children together forgiveness could not work like that. It was hard to pull down inside to actually mean it. True forgiveness occurs after you are able to speak about an offense and no longer feel the pain it caused you once before. Unforgiveness leaves you in a state of replaying and reliving the same emotions, internal damage, stress, and state of mind you encountered the first time the offense happened. Therefore, forgiveness is ultimately for you, not the offender. In order for me to move forward, I had to learn to forgive not only my offenders' offense but also myself as the Lord was revealing who I really was as a person. It was a long journey but ultimately through the strength of the Lord and the power of the Holy Ghost, I'm coming out on the other side victorious.

Here's the deal-breaker, once I completely conquer forgiveness there's an entirely new world that I have to learn to exist in. This world includes new normals not only related to the pandemic but dealing with the mental anguish, discomfort, and confusion of my children. There is a new era of singleness that is quite different than 20 years ago and I'm walking in this world with the innocent yet naive dating age of 23. This is a seriously crazy yet eye-opening journey, but we can get into more detail about that in my new and upcoming book.

Chapter 6
Crush Syndrome

It has been reported that in the case of a sudden collapse of an eight-story building, 80% of the entrapped victims instantly die by the direct effects of trauma, 10% survive with minor trauma, while 10% are badly injured; of those, 7/10 develop crush syndrome. That explains why I felt as if I barely made it out alive. There was an undeniable pressure that I tried to grin and bear through but it was obvious the 20% survival rate still left me injured. The old coping techniques were not as effective as they used to be. I looked healthy on the outside but was dying on the inside. Stress is a silent killer and as mentioned earlier I began to experience an unfamiliar response which was anxiety and depression. Earlier in the book, I also explained Gennelle's story. Gennelle's posture was completely uncomfortable but if her body was not bent in a certain way but lying flat I really believe she may not have come out alive. As you may recall, her legs were crossed underneath her, with her right arm pinned and she could only move her left arm. Although we find ourselves in some uncomfortable positions during this journey I would argue that they have kept us alive. Allowing us to get oxygen, maintain temperature, and adequate overflow of the living water.

Crush syndrome, according to Dr. Tejsrhi Shah of Medecins Sans Frontieres, says that crush syndrome is the outcome of when tissue is compressed and dies. When the pressure is released, a buildup of toxins from the muscle breakdown floods the body and it is unable to cope. If you are situated in the right position the debris of life will not crush you. I was determined not to take any anti-anxiety or antidepressant medication in the fear of addiction or dependence. I am not advocating for anyone reading this book to neglect help or avoid the advice of any medical professional. I'm just telling my story. I found myself to be on my face a lot crying to God, in my closet on the floor, on my knees praying, with my bible open more, and surrounding myself with people who spoke about life, restoration, and growth. God surrounded me with new people. These people began to identify things in me that God had deposited and started pushing me in the direction of whom I really was. However, all things can appear to be a life jacket in the middle of a storm. I can't deny that I felt stubbornness and anger as I wanted to stay where I was so I could drown in my misery. My world as I knew it had not only been crumbled but the aftershocks of the destruction were beginning to appear.

Once the foundation was broken, the Lord showed me the dirt that looked like water waves circulating under and over with a great deal of visible debris. It was the ground we built our life on. Yes, you got the house, the cars, two boys, two girls, the husband but underneath it all there was a great deal of anger, abuse, ungodliness, and the witchcraft spirit of control and rebelliousness operating in the home. Not only was it in me but I saw the effects of it in my children. There was pain that was never dealt with as a family even before the divorce. My misconception of a marriage, the ability to adapt, ignore, not feel or even love because I had no clue what it looked like to allow me to contribute to the pain my children suffered behind closed doors. We appeared to be a ready-made family but I can say a smile is not what it always appears to be. There were so many secrets right under my nose. I cannot say that the Holy Spirit never tried to reveal anything to me. I'm guilty of putting man and the idea of the so longed-for family before God. I had very few

Transforming Into Disasters Worst Enemy

dreams that I remember but one that I did have about my youngest daughter kept recurring. I gave up seeking the reason for that dream in my laziness as she was always so happy. Now, I'm really awake. I see exactly what it was about. Studies have shown that children who experience repeated and severe abuse growing up suffer impairment in their ability to complete normal developmental tasks. This in turn leads to deficits in their ability to self-soothe, trust, and view the world as a safe place. Poor judgment, varying degrees of paranoia, self-sabotage, and impaired problem-solving skills follow them into adulthood. All of the above describes my mother but my daughter does not wrestle with what statistics say. Through the grace of God, we are able to still find healing, restoration, and my daughter's destiny will not be aborted as the devil had planned. We will get into that in my upcoming book. The good news is that generational curses are being replaced with generational blessings as the Bible says in Psalms 112:2 The seeds of the righteous will be mighty in the land.

    I witnessed mistreatment and unnecessary behavior yet made excuses that my oldest daughter and son are now having to face and deal with as adults. I coward out and left our emotions unprotected and unguided many times. Trying to make it up with having fun, gifts, and a journal I gave my son during his teenage years. I told him, "This is your journal, I know you are hurt and harboring a lot of anger. You are free to write anything you feel in this book. You can cuss, fuss, scream and cry your words out here and you will never get into trouble for it." Let's just say, I peeked in it one time and this boy can cuss like a sailor. All jokes aside, the journal was a nice gesture but it never brought a solution to the pain. Once again, the misconception of marriage led me to believe submitting was even when it hurts. I feel so stupid and weak. I prayed all of the time even to the point of bringing the family together as if I was the head, so we could pray together as a family. But it was more ritualistic because nobody really wanted to be in the circle, but me. If I was really walking in who God called me to be, that devil would have been exposed and evicted a lot sooner.

    I know I keep talking about the pain someone else caused but I caused pain on my children as well. The divorce has introduced counseling in our lives and all of my children agree that I wasn't as great a mother as I once believed. It's a hard pill to swallow but I can say it has given me something to go to the Lord about and inquire about specific instructions on how to change. Not that I'm all so great because I'm not. See,

Transforming Into Disasters Worst Enemy

perfection comes when you allow the perfectionist to operate, move and abide in your life. You always have time to fix any relationship and to change as long as there is air in your body. My children said I yelled a lot, never listened to them, and did not love them the way they needed to be loved. I also was yelled at a lot, never heard, and did not feel loved. Wow, that could have also been my problem as a wife, wait, a friend, sister, and coworker. I learned that just because they all were born out of the same womb they still had different personal needs and I may have allowed some valuable time escape that could have been detrimental to the building of their character or guidance to their destiny. Thanks be unto God that He said that He will restore the time that the locust and cankerworm ate up! No time lost because a thousand years is like a day to God. I prayed and the Lord showed me how to treat, praise, discipline, love and, most of all, how to get them to their individual destinies because they were assigned to me. These little people the Lord blessed me with are astonishing people who are going to affect the world for the greater good.

    The exposure, pain, shame, and process of healing nearly crushed me but God would not let me go. Crush syndrome can cause hypovolemic shock or hyperkalemia due to the sequestration of water in the injured muscle and the release of cellular potassium by the muscle. I know it sounds like another language but just know, it's not good and almost impossible to reverse. The shock of the infidelity was enormous and its mission was to deplete the water (Spirit of God) I already had stored up. In addition, to release bitterness, anger, and unforgiveness in my heart to ultimately destroy my destiny putting me at risk for spiritual dehydration.

    This situation like sin can lead to other destructive outcomes. Hypovolemic shock and hyperkalemia eventually lead to a medical term called metabolic acidosis which is the release of cellular phosphate and sulphate by the injured muscle cells. Wait, it gets worse because the body was designed to keep working, as the blood continues to circulate the toxicity that was released now filters through the kidneys. This now leads to acute kidney injury or disseminated intravascular coagulation (DIC) which is considered a medical emergency. The body loses the ability to clot the blood resulting in bleeding out which then leads to death. The kidneys play key roles in the body not only by filtering the blood and getting rid of waste products, but also by balancing the electrolyte levels in the body, controlling blood pressure, and stimulating the production of red blood cells. You mean to tell me the kidneys not only filter but balance and produce?

This season of my life seemed as if I was operating with one functioning kidney instead of two. The idea of operating as a single parent and the reality of it was completely opposite. Here are some harsh truths about the waste, balance, and production of the area of parenting I had to face. The wastes built up because of my own negligence to face and deal with them, so here I stand filtering through years and years of waste. Trying to restore the blood and salvage the kidney at the same time is quite a challenge. My children and I had become so complacent in the dysfunction of existing and not living that we had no clue on what to do next. Our level of dysfunction was in just being present and not interacting. Life was robotic and unfruitful. I really thought I had reached the peak of my existence and was living my best life. Now I realize my life has just begun as well as my children. It hurts but once they realize our best is yet to come they will be able to accept the truth that although the past is what built us there is so much more the Lord has in store for us. We began the process of filtering out the waste with professional counselors, church, prayer, talking, crying, fighting, and learning ourselves. In learning who I really was, it gave me the

Theresa Padgett

ability to filter out the woman I created, or should I say who I allowed my environment to tell me I was. I always say it's not who they call you but what you answer to. You can call me a bitch all day but if I don't answer, respond or acknowledge it, I have extinguished the power you thought you had in labeling me.

The balancing of the court documented joint custody of our children was something I never saw us having to do. We were supposed to be that solid example of that couple with longevity of love, raising our children together from the womb until they left home, sending each out one by one to begin their own life. Living life and enjoying one another in our empty nest. However, I'm learning to embrace the beauty of not my will but thy will be done. This change affected us all, but some of us are deeper than others. This new way of adaptation carries some necessary tears and heartache. You heard right, the tears and heartache are evidence that the Lord is restoring love. If you remember there are many traumatic occurrences that I don't remember crying about. So now the Lord is removing old faulty mechanisms used to survive to introduce me to a new world of healthy mechanisms to aid in my healing. Although I'm not completely there, this is a good start.

Transforming Into Disasters Worst Enemy

So now I'm going to work everyday, carrying the family through the pandemic, cooking, cleaning, staying on top of the kids' education, and paying the bills. Wait a minute, all of this doesn't look all that unfamiliar. The sad truth is that our family has been operating with only one kidney the entire time. Not saying I did it all by myself but operating as the head covering all of the above seemed to be my normal. Why am I so stressed out? Is it because the harsh reality is sending me into shock? Shock is when the circulatory system fails and ultimately leads to organ failure resulting in death. Understanding the difference between reality and the fantasy that I had made myself believe something that was not true. Going through this divorce left me in a position that I began questioning the entire 17 years of our marriage. This fool had a secret account, a secret phone, a secret lover or lovers, and here I was believing that both parties were operating in loyalty, honor, and respect.

In infidelity, trust is the first thing to go and the last thing to come back. Does that mean that trust starts over a new one if you divorce which by default frees you from having to trust that individual again? Will I ever be able to trust anyone again? You will find out in my new book. Will I become self-sabotaging or self-restored? I faced physical abuse in prior relationships before my marriage but this financial abuse and emotional neglect is a deceptive little bastard. So obvious but yet so quiet. So quiet yet so destructive. As the veil was removed, I was allowed to see what was really going on in this little house on a prairie. Stress hormones affect your digestion, immunity, & sleep patterns. Adrenalin works by preparing you for vigorous physical activity but also reduces your appetite which leads to loss of weight. I dropped from 150lbs to a solid 135lbs within a few months. Body's stress response is usually self-limiting and will return to normal if the threat has passed. It appears that even after the divorce there was a low, subtle tremble in my cells as we continued this healing process. My attitude began to reflect the stress I was dealing with and I was able to go see a doctor to get some time off of work, refusing to accept any pharmacological therapy as mentioned earlier. When stressors are always present, a person feels constantly under attack. Already being stubborn, I noticed all of my negative thoughts were magnified and the anger fuse was short. When Fight/Flight stays on overexposure to cortisol and other stress hormones eventually begin to destroy the body. There is an increased risk of anxiety, depression, digestive, weight interruptions, sleep problems, heart disease, headaches, memory, and concentration impairment. I began to experience the anxiety, depression, and sleep problems that it wasn't long before I was so stressed out that I started having memory and concentration impairment. My mind was always going and remained full even if it was just racing thoughts. Do we remain like this or do we become disaster's worst enemy while underneath the rubble?

Chapter 7
Determination

Reflecting over the years, I can admit I have fought harder for the good of others only to have stopped, looked back, and seen that the person I was fighting for has stopped fighting a long time ago. One question a person would need to ask after any traumatic situation is if I really want to overcome, not can I overcome this. The answer is that you can overcome anything if you are determined to get to that other side where healing and restoration is present. Fear of the process is what causes doubt and confusion. Some may feel as if it is not worth all of the hard work, they are not strong enough, too traumatized to heal or even just may not want to. I know it sounds odd but there are people who like to live in self-pity, misery, and defeat. Hopefully, after getting this far in my book your faith has been strengthened and if you once dealt with hesitance to fight for any reason you

Transforming Into Disasters Worst Enemy

are now equipped with consciousness, firepower, and pertinacity to become disaster's worst enemy!

After the pain had lingered so long, I began to compare my emotionally traumatic situation with those who suffered physical traumatic injuries. I knew I had to continue to live and I wanted to overcome this but how? This would take more than just praying, trusting, and believing the Lord. What was my part in the process? What causes a person to get back on a skateboard once planting their face on the concrete after attempting to perform a triple kick flip on a stair rail? Ouch! Sounds painful but those athletes are resilient and it's not long before you see them right back on the rails again.

How about a car accident? There are many people who have a hard time getting back behind the wheel after a car accident but many people are looking to get their car repaired so they can get back on the road. No matter the danger, the time it took to heal, or even the risk of other drivers that are on the road. Let me pause right there. Although I walk through the valley of the shadow of death I will fear no evil because Thou art with me... Wanting to move on but paralyzed with the fear of knowing the danger that awaits and not wanting to go through any more processes to heal. Thou art with me. The most profound part is willing to be vulnerable to other drivers who are on the road of your life. Thou art with me. You know what I'm talking about. Just because people are issued a license does not mean that they are careful with the equipment. Do you realize that in Nevada vehicular manslaughter is defined as the proximate cause of the death of another person through the act or omission that constitutes simple negligence? It is treated as a misdemeanor unless the driver is under the influence of alcohol, drugs, or driving recklessly. It is not considered murder but the outcome of the victim does not change. There's the splinter! If I open up my heart again the outcome could be the same if not even worse. Risking repeated offense versus true happiness. Living in a constant protective state is more nerve-wracking than just being free. Here's the nugget. It is considered murder but the outcome of the victim does not change unless the victim takes back the power of being labeled a victim and changes it into being a conqueror. Now, the results of a victim cannot measure up to who I am as a conqueror! I'm way too high to be a victim any longer. When the trials of life begin to bring in worry, fear or doubt I remind those trials that I am free and whom the Son has set free is free indeed.

Transforming Into Disasters Worst Enemy

Determination is a firm or fixed intention to achieve a desired end. I am determined to be free and live life more abundantly. I will not be in bondage to my past.

The most life-threatening example that I remember researching was shark bites after being awakened one night by the noise on the television. I saw a man on the television going through rehabilitation after having limb removal surgery due to a shark bite. I found myself intrigued with the interview as they went into detail about the attack. He discussed the sudden blow that came out of nowhere and the overwhelming fear of losing his life he experienced as he was involuntarily going under water in his own circle of blood. He was traumatized beyond measure. I could only relate as it sounded so familiar as to what I was experiencing. I even shed a few tears as he told how all he ever wanted to do as a kid was surf and how safe he felt when he was in the water. Now, just as with my marriage, it will never be the same. I too know what it feels like to have dreams as a child that you thought were coming true only to realize that there was never a happy ending. In relation to the sudden blow, there was a twist in the story. Here I am in my brokenness and trauma, looking at a man who was also broken and traumatized. The interviewer asked, "Well, are you going to ever get back into the water?" He answered, "Without a doubt...I cannot wait to get back in the water." Large emoji eyes! What possessed him to answer that question like that? Are you kidding me? Why are you going back in to let him finish you off? He said he would not be satisfied with just giving up and had to conquer his fear in order to live again. I could not believe it. I began to think about all of the fears that were going through my mind. All of the things that were prohibiting me to live again. To get back out there and go another round. Determination comes from the inside and it takes a great deal of courage to operate in it. It is like that courage you muster up right before diving into a pool off of a 6ft diving board. Or I'm sorry, a lot of us, I said, cannot relate to that. How about pushing through stage fright when having to stand in front of an audience or walking into a job interview consisting of three-panel interviewers. But being determined to reach the reward on the other side is what pushes you. What is the reward if I chose to be an overcomer and not a victim? What am I showing my children? What statement am I making to other women? I'm determined to make it not just for me but for other women who may share some parts of my story young and old alike. Neglecting not to extend this encouragement to men. We all have a past that we have to deal with in the present so we all can share a better future. The takeaway is to have the courage to get back in there but notice the rehabilitation he had to go through in order to successfully get back in the water. Sometimes we don't have the problem with getting back out there but we jump out unprepared. Listen to God, you will know the how and most importantly the when.

Bethany Hamilton is a brave woman who was attacked by a 14-foot tiger shark at the age of 13. She lost her left arm but not her heart as a result of the attack. She ended up returning to the water a short one month time frame after the attack. She then returned to surfing and within two years had won her first national surfing title. Bethany told the interviewer, "If I was like a person that just quit surfing after this, I wouldn't be a real surfer. I'm definitely going to get back in the water." How motivating, she said if she would have allowed this tragedy to stop her from surfing then she would not be a real surfer. It wasn't the attack that caused her to win her first national surfing title or brought fame to her name. It was because of her undefeated spirit. She made a decision that she was a surfer no matter what may have tried to stop that. What are your unfortunate circumstances communicating to you? What's more important is, what are you communicating in those circumstances. I had to make up my mind that defeat was not an option and it was not over until God said it was over. The truth is if I decided to quit I wouldn't be a winner. The Bible tells me I am more than a conqueror through Jesus Christ.

Disappointment is an opportunity for spiritual growth. First thing to realize is we set expectations for people in our lives and once those expectations are not met we become disappointed. Here's my struggle, the only expectation that I had for my other half was not to ever cheat on me, never have an outside relationship with another woman, never confide or tell your darkest secrets to any other woman except with me. Me, me, me, me…. Why was it more of a struggle for me to face a challenge from another woman and not express any concerns about the family, a husband having a relationship with the Lord, being all the way in and truthful to the entire family, meeting the families emotional needs, building and supporting everything God wants for us? Yes, infidelity is and always will be unacceptable in this past and any future relationship I will encounter but the real cut came from my own insecurities. With my mouth I can say I was great, I had the mind, body, and spirit, there's nobody like me, etc. But did I really believe it? Sometimes people want you weak, timid, and isolated so they can keep you in a box especially when you lack the yield signs of self-respect, confidence or self-love. When you house those on the inside it illuminates on the outside to those who purposely prey on the broken. However, I was willing to live there because I was comfortable. That's exactly how the enemy got in during my healing process. It's funny how this same spirit keeps coming for me. Even now as my current circumstances are trying to keep me in bondage I'm realizing there's something in me that's allowing this monster to constantly get in to operate in my life. But now it's evident that learning is occurring because now as quick as it invades the faster it's exposed and I'm determined to defeat this chapter once and for all.

There was a process that led to this determination. It just did not happen overnight. As mentioned earlier in this book, there was a great deal of soul searching, managing the divorce side effects of myself, the children, and what I would like to discuss "Phantom healing." Phantom healing is the opposite of what phantom pain is defined as. Phantom pain is feeling pain or sensation in a limb that no longer exists either by amputation or an accident. The bottom line is that it is no longer there but because the mind cannot process the loss of the limb it still feels it. There was a time while I was going through this process I was convinced that I was completely healed. After spending a year still present after the offense I believed I had gone through the process and once I announced my decision to follow through with the divorce I was ready. Everyone else had to catch up with me, so I believed. Pretending to be healed and actually being healed are two different realities. Some preachers have taught us that if you speak it long enough you will believe it. I began to speak it so much that my words started uncovering the veil more and more. The truth was becoming more and more evident because no matter what was coming out of my mouth my eyes would see otherwise.

For someone who encouraged marriage, counseled others to fight, I didn't look at marriage the same anymore. In the hurt mentality, I worked through real forgiveness but not the forgiveness adopted by my past poor coping mechanisms. My mind would revisit the thoughts of infidelity and the understanding that people make mistakes even if it's as harsh as lies, betrayal, deception, and even what we had experienced. If these things should easily be overlooked, I wondered, "Why even commit?" Why get married? We treat marriage as having a glorified boyfriend or girlfriend that we can so easily break up with. My mind began to doubt true covetousness and the beauty of it all together. I got a taste of reality and it was bitter. Sexual deception is not simply a violation of trust or something women need to get over. When a woman is reacting to sexual betrayal it's because two necessary needs were violated. Safety and truth were removed and as I stated earlier, first to go and last to come back. There were three things I had to get in check so determination could fully mature. I had to find safety and truth in Jesus. I have to overcome my thoughts and finally, I have to be transparent.

The first person I had to stop depending on was myself. What do you mean? It wasn't through my own strength, a self-proclaimed process, or any ideas I created to get me through this painful process. If it was up to me, I would have quite a long time ago. I was governed by stubbornness, pride, and an array of unstable emotions. Trauma changes the way we see people in the world around us. It unravels our sense of safety and even changes the way we feel about ourselves. Unseen wounds poison us from the inside out and if left untreated could destroy us. My grandmother's cause of death was gangrene. She neglected to give the appropriate attention to a small wound on her leg. Just like emotional wounds the gangrene poisoned her body. Likewise to the need for air, water, and temperature regulation while under the ashes or rubble. Remember, if those three essential items are overlooked or neglected for too long death could occur. Healing for the trauma we deal with is important for a healthy mind, body, and Spirit. Only God can heal from the inside out. My way of healing was with a wine bottle because I was too scared to try anything else. Looking for it in other relationships was all human dependence and it even caused me to not only disobey God but degrade myself. Dealing with constant anxiety, fear, unpredictable emotions, and inability to trust, loss, personal guilt, shame, and most harmful anger. The anger was causing me to steer away from that happy, joking, and always smiling woman who lit up every room. I became easily irritated, snapping, and mean-hearted. This situation was like walking into an angry nest of wasps. A honeybee can only sting once and then it dies. A wasp's stinger remains intact so it can sting over and over again. I was walking in denial of mine and my children's reality and was literally walking wounded. Thinking I had it all together and had nothing to learn from this situation but I was wrong.

Many people who have served lengthy sentences in prison were able to survive because they never allowed their minds to be behind bars. Locked up but not in bondage. Imagine living in a world absolutely unbothered? Reminds me of Paul in the Bible. A great man who did his best work behind bars. He said, "...for which I suffer trouble as an evildoer, even to the point of chains; but the word of God is not chained." Freedom of the mind is a powerful place to be and being able to live in that place disarms all weapons formed against you. In order to overcome the thoughts in my mind, I had to first realize who I was. I never realized I was created for more than a wife and a mother. There was a queen of great royalty, poise yet humbleness that I never allowed the world to meet. It was time for me to be who God created me to be, not who I thought I was. When will you start believing that God created you for greatness? That you actually do have a purpose for your existence? I reached a level of comfortability and plateaued at just being mediocre. Yes, the dog, house, car, and family are the American dream but it means nothing if I just get mine and leave a dying world without ever attempting to encourage anyone to do great things. Walking this true Christian walk had put a strain on my marriage and confused my children about the significance of their spiritual walk. I have to admit my girls ended up enjoying prayer, church service, and activities more than my boys due to the examples they were following. I'm speaking a great deal about this because being unequally yoked can cause a shift of unbalance in the children. What do I mean? The kids lean more towards the parents' behavior that they find more comfortable for them. A donkey and an ox could not be yoked together because a donkey is stubborn. A donkey does what it wants but an ox moves on command in obedience. What does that mean, in the efforts of a better explanation, let's just use the metaphor of a donkey as the flesh and the ox as the spirit of God. You can have two people come together to raise a family and they both are led by two different things. Eventually, the donkey will get hurt because the ox is so strong it will be forced to move or the ox will remain still and get nothing done. I was 23 years old at the time and it's fair to ask the question, "What do you really know at that age?" However, I am recommending any and everyone who reads this book to really evaluate that question in the midst of marriage preparation. Study your partner and, most of all, study yourself. As I have mentioned before, I will not sit here and say that I regret my previous marriage because we did at one time love one another, have great times and we had some beautiful children together.

As mentioned earlier, my children began to deal with the divorce one year after I had already gone through most of the grieving processes. It was as if it just happened to them and as they are all different in personalities they also dealt with loss in a different manner. I tried everything, prayer, counseling, suffocating them with love, my time, communication, silence, you name it. We spent several months transitioning from me and the girls sleeping in one room at my friend's house to us moving into a new home with one parent. There were so many changes in such a short duration of time and we all had to adjust whether we wanted to or not. My youngest daughter switched to a new school and it was so difficult for her. Our home became more and more toxic as all of our underlying personal issues began to surface, the healing process and realization of our new reality became clear. I spent more time trying to deal with things behind closed doors than out in the open. Trying to protect them from my pain, hurt and transformation thinking I was doing them a favor. It was backfiring because every time they realized life would never be the same and life was not as cake as we made it; we would have these big blowups in the house. It was time to understand the only way my children would heal is if I stopped hiding during the healing process. How else would they know that healing was a process and it's not pretty if I just show up one day all better without revealing that there was ever a process, to begin with. The metamorphosis of caterpillars in a cocoon is left up to your imagination. As we really cannot see inside the cocoon physically. We only can see inside the cocoon once the process is over and the cocoon opens up. What do we see? No residue of the metamorphosis nor the struggle that the butterfly experienced to come out. It serves as an injustice to our children for them to believe that the process of healing is beautiful. That it never hurts, is easy, or will never be a struggle to get there. Transparency is a hard yet necessary reality. It is the realness of it that makes it effective. My children began to reveal some things about myself that were hard to accept and vice versa. Although there were plenty of nights of debating, screaming, and crying ultimately accountability and change became the silver lining. A point at which I thought we would never reach. Although a work in progress we have come a long way since the beginning.

Transforming Into Disasters Worst Enemy

As we were all walking through this together I realized how important it was for me to lock-in, be steadfast, immovable, and always abounding. I could not stop fighting. The scripture actually quotes, "...steadfast, immovable and always abounding in the work of the Lord, knowing that your labor is not in vain in the Lord." These little people were God's precious souls. We were never alone during this entire process and I realized the Lord wants the glory out of our lives. I was determined to make disaster my worst enemy.

Disaster is defined as a sudden event, such as an accident or a natural catastrophe, that causes great damage or loss of life. Analyzing that definition leads me to recognize the word "sudden." Why sudden? Without warning, quickly, unexpectedly. That makes sense. No one really is prepared for disaster. That is the first bullet of disaster. When it occurs the surprise factor is the first and yet hardest reality to accept. Therefore, just like an enemy or a thief who will never announce themselves to you, disaster will enter your life relentlessly unannounced. In relation to an enemy, who means no good, disaster is too my enemy. Now that the rubble and ashes barricade me as a result of the disaster, it is now that I return the favor. That's right, not laying down to die, I am being strengthened to come out of the heavy rubble stronger than ever. As the enemy comes to kill, steal and destroy when that plan has failed all efforts are in vain. Disaster, you too will be defeated because what you meant for evil my God will turn around for good! Not only am I victorious but now I'm coming for you. I see what you tried to do to my children, my mind, body, and Spirit. Like a bomb that destroys a direct place, the radon or residue of destruction can be effective for miles and miles around. Touching, causing pain, sickness, and even death to everything in its path. I have now "Transformed into disaster's worst enemy while under the rubble."

Chapter 8
Will to Live

It is important to realize that feelings of failure, defeat, and giving up do not translate into weakness. You are not Superman or Superwoman, therefore, your ability to have superpowers are seriously obsolete. Being that God made you a human, you house these mind-blowing responses called emotions. I know, completely opposite of what the world calls strength. The world wants you to not feel and ultimately to trust in your own ways. Eventually, if we continue to self-medicate with drugs, alcohol, sex, unhealthy relationships, gambling, and all of these other distractions that steer us away from dealing with the issue at hand we will be unable to feel the necessary stages of grief that lead to healthy healing. It is one thing to allow emotions to govern your life in an impulsive state or to use them as God has designed them to be which your internal compass is. You will know what is right, wrong, safe, dangerous, happy, sad, angry, real, or fake just by what your emotions tell you. In a healthy mind frame, emotions become tools in weighing out a choice versus allowing emotions to be the choice. Read that again. How many of us still made risky decisions even when it didn't feel right? Or contrary, have avoided what appeared to be a good decision because it felt like the right thing to do. Ultimately, you have the final decision. God does not force Himself on us as He gives us free will and that is the toughest area to master in adulting.

Not processing the stages of grief effectively can cause delayed and sometimes healing avoidance altogether. Feelings of failure, defeat, and giving up are the beginning stages of the depression phase in the grieving process. In my introduction, the young lady, Gennelle, who had been underneath the rubble in the twin towers expedited through the grieving phases in a matter of hours unlike the normal process. I would even argue that she may have skipped some phases and accepted to remain homestead at some phases such as acceptance of her life ending there. Have you ever noticed yourself giving up and accepting a fate of death and destruction? I can say that I have on several occasions because I could not see the direction in which God was leading me. I'm too stubborn to remain homestead in defeat. However, the exhaustion of

Transforming Into Disasters Worst Enemy

fighting constantly is beginning to wear me out. What now?

Seeking counseling opened my eyes up. In lieu of sitting with myself showed me an ugly reality that made me want to bury myself deeper under the rubble. Let me be honest, I believe I hold some responsibility for the failure of my family and the misconstrued concepts and behavior in my children. Just wanting a chance to fix it all but this time I can't fix it. I have to let go and accept the fact that I have absolutely no control. No control over what happens to them, how they process life, or feel about me. Everyone who tells me something that I don't like about myself angers me beyond measure and I begin to shut them out. I see why people choose to be alone but do that address the inconsistencies or flaws I harbor. No worries, no accountability or responsibility. Wouldn't that be the perfect world? Or will it be the cop-out world? I will admit that this book has been therapeutic for me. I've never cried so much talking about myself. As I've gone deeper to share my life with all of you wonderful people I began to dig up some answers to this questionable world I've lived in for so many years. There were more skeletons in my closet than in my marriage. Wow… now that's some facts. Perhaps, having dealt with those skeletons before the initiation of my family could have saved us from a great deal of heartache. Hoping my life will be a testimony at which someone will be healed, delivered, or set free. Realizing my horrible coping techniques, inability to love myself or any other human being, reflecting and accepting the truth of my past has brought me to a place of questioning my real purpose. Who am I really? Do those around me really experience love from me or have I poisoned those around me with my distorted expressions of love? Now the question is, how will this pass down to the next generation or will it? In a place of disappointment and shame, I realize that I am responsible for either bringing them out or leaving them in captivity. So today I choose blessings not curses. Nobody knows like I know how I wish I found these things out about myself decades ago. Who have I been measuring myself up to? Who was my role model or did I think I had it all figured out? I don't want anybody to have pity love for me but whoever I connect to is going to have to understand my entirety and realize this new posture in my life God is first. Prayerfully, that too will be his posture no exceptions. Also including the sensitivity and the God-seeking instructions on how to handle a woman like me. Most want to pretend but that sheep's clothing will get heavy

Transforming Into Disasters Worst Enemy

and sooner or later that wolf's snout will have to come out for air.

For every cause, there is an effect and vice versa. If you touch fire the effect is a burn. In the event that the burn occurs and it angers me, do I have the right to be angry at the fire? The fire was only operating in what it was created to do. At some point, I have to assume some responsibility for how my hand got in the fire in the first place. As I have been reflecting over the last couple of years, I have come to grips that the effects of my life today cannot be blamed on the divorce itself. These treacherous situations are coming out as a result of the divorce but were not caused by the divorce. They were already there before the divorce and were only free to surface because the created normalcy was disrupted. It was time to deal with some hard truths. The divorce only came to do what a divorce does, which is to dissolve a union. That means that everything underneath the marriage was uncovered and now visible for not only the eye to see but the mind and heart to deal with. The lies were dissolved. The fake smiles were dissolved. The happy family picture story was dissolved.

As much as I love pictures, certain timeframes to view them is like a stab in my heart. I now view pictures differently. Years ago, I would admire the faces, the color schemes, how we felt that day and even remembered stories such as where we ate as a family afterward, the funny things and difficulty we had agreeing on one pose, and so on. Horace said, "A picture is a poem without words." I believe that is completely true as we all can look at pictures and read a different story. What's your story? What have others told you while looking in from the outside? Is the majority accurate? Let me tell you something, whether they are or not, don't live your story based on other people's interpretations. A person may look and say, "Oh, my goodness, look how happy they are." Others may even try to frame you into what they want you to be. Framing in photography refers to the technique of drawing focus to the subject in the photo by blocking other parts of the image with something in the scene. When others do it they want you to only focus on them or their agenda, their vision so you ignore the surrounding factors like your responsibility to your family, yourself, and even more importantly, God. Blocking out reality, as I was so successful at doing, brought me to a place of being so far detached from myself that I am relearning who I am. Someone asked me what I like doing and I found it strange to have to sit and ponder on that answer. Why don't I have anything that I enjoy doing? What have I done? I've been so busy pleasing everyone else that I neglected to take care of myself. I am not advising one to live a selfish, self-centered life but take some time to love on you sometimes. The kids will eat and your house can look like someone lives there because it's actually true.

I look at those same pictures after knowing all that I know about what was really happening during those time frames and they hurt my heart to look at. I looked in my ex-husband's face and wonder was he cheating during that time, did he really love me, or if he even wanted to be there? Then I would individually look into my children's eyes and wonder if they were oblivious to the trauma they experienced or if it really felt normal to them. Were they really happy? Then I would see my big smiling face and realize how empty I really was. How blind I was to the truth and how selfishly happy I was to finally have a family and not even ask anyone else if they were happy. I was satisfied with having a house full of children who all looked alike as I always wanted and how we were so proud to be a family who survived the westside and kept momma and daddy under one roof. Pride comes before destruction. Was God really reverenced in our home, in our lives? I didn't ask if the gospel of Jesus Christ was never taught in our home because I personally did that. I'm asking if this Bible was actually

Theresa Padgett

a way of life, who we were, and what was rooted in our babies? Absolutely not, and I hold equal responsibility to that truth. Now that I know the cause I need to learn how to respond to the effect. Blaming and harassing them for their lack of understanding of how to live holy is not the answer. It's time that I truly pastor my children and throw away the idea of parenting them. Who really knows how to parent anyway? In order to lead them to Jesus, I have to bring their attention to God's hand in every situation. It's important to unveil God's unconditional love, grace, and mercy. Live by example and tell stories of my past, in return, showing them that I am not as holy as they believe I portray to be but I am forgiven and changed. Children see you as you are today and it's almost impossible for them to believe that you have done what if not worse than what they do today. The unspoken picture of perfection illuminates a false reality that secretly holds standards above our children's heads. In return, leaving them with low self-esteem, feelings of worthlessness, hopelessness, defeat, and failure. It's just as bad as not processing through the stages of grief appropriately however what is that they should be grieving? One would argue, "I never told my child that they have to be perfect," equating it to self-inflicted pain. The contrary is that you never told them that failure is a part of life and we as parents have left those self-perceived thoughts there to fester, take root, and poison our children, equating to involuntary pain.

Let's talk about self-inflicted pain vs involuntary pain. Self-inflicted pain is what we cause on ourselves yet the involuntary pain is what others cause on us. It's hard to wrap our minds around the fact that I have a lot to do with the behavior, responses, and thought processes of this young person in front of me. My friends, family and I share situations about our children all the time and I can count on one hand if we ever admitted that any disrespectful, rebellious or disobedient behavior was a result of what we have done or the lack thereof. I can personally say that I have not. This new area in my life has allowed me to realize who I really am and some areas of myself are not all that beautiful even today as I am writing this book. It's unfortunate that it took all of this for me to meet the real me. On the opposite spectrum of this, as I allow God to clean that person up, I am meeting a Queen who is a business owner, nurse, dancer, author, preacher, teacher, intercessory prayer warrior, amazing mother, and a wife who is undeniably his good thing. An elegant, caring, selfless, and compassionate person who now looks through the lenses of not her own but

Theresa Padgett

God's eyes. I am a collaborator with others to empower themselves mentally, emotionally, spiritually and physically. What if I would have given up and resisted the change that I stubbornly attempted to do on so many occasions? If I ever get married again, this time, it will be forever because I know who I am and who I can be to him. I wasn't horrible but I could have been better. My children are fortunately in a position to benefit from the change and I pray I am an example that God can do anything but fail.

    The disaster did what disaster does; however, the enemy wanted the effects to destroy all that I am, my destiny, and everything attached to me. Like Gennelle, when she made up her mind to live, she began to talk to herself and God met her right where she was and began to minister to her through an angel. Talking to yourself may be the only reasonable human voice you will hear. There is power in the ability to choose. Now unto Him who is able to do exceedingly and abundantly above all, we could ever ask or think according to the power that works in me. I choose to live and not just live but to live that more abundantly. These aren't just familiar scriptures but a way of life. If she would have chosen to die I'm pretty sure she would have died. The mind, being the computer system, would have agreed and controlled the entire body to eventually shut down. I've seen it so many times in the field that I work. Once a patient decides it is over or gives up, it's not very long before they transition.

The dictionary defines free will as the power of acting without the constraint of necessity or fate; the ability to act at one's own discretion. However, in this Christian walk, we have the responsibility to choose right, making us accountable for our choice. So the truth is there is an underlying constraint which is the Holy Spirit at which we understand that all things are permissible but all things are not beneficial. It's our internal law enforcer but I can admit to having ignored it on several occasions. What about fate? Do you believe that some outcomes come into existence because of fate? While studying fate, it seems as if it is a will, principal, or destiny, almost as if fate is a person or an entity. Further in my study I am unable to find the word fate in the King James Version; however, destiny can reasonably interchange with the word fate. I'm still not satisfied… as I dig a little deeper on fate as the word sounds mystical I came upon another interesting finding. The reason I wanted to dig deeper is because I understand that both destiny and fate are defined as the cause of an inevitable and often adverse outcome, condition, or end. My question is if so then why is fate not mentioned and destiny is mentioned in the KJV of the bible, for example as related to predestined and destined? This is important because if fate and destiny are the same yet driven by different forces they will have different outcomes in my life. Did you hear me? What's the driving force in your life? As many will have an idea in the direction they want to go in life but if you allow other people or even yourself to drive the outcome will be different. God may have a detour, a different route, a rest period, or believe it or not, a different destination on which your heart is set. Now the truth remains to test the spirit by the spirit as it will do me no good to believe all spirits are the same. There, in ignorance, one can be deceived even unto the point of death. Finally, I came to the conclusion that fates are defined as the three goddesses, Atropos, Clotho, and Lachesis, who determine the course of human life in classical mythology. That's why it did not sit well in my spirit. It's not by fate that I walk but by faith that I walk. So, I ask again, do you think that some outcomes come into existence because of fate? Fate is determined by another spirit and my answer is no; however, if it is my destiny as called into existence when I was in my mother's womb like Jeremiah as a reference in Jeremiah 1:5 then that's what it is.

In conclusion, my will if I live by the Spirit will align with God's will and my prayer is that the two are in agreement and are pleasing to the Lord. Thy will be done and thy kingdom come on earth as it is in heaven. I can't be the only one who feels that way. There was an undeniable urge for me to come out of the rubble victorious. I cannot die here, there is too much for me to do. Millions of people exodus are assigned to my hands. Women will find out where they have allowed the frame to blind them from the entire picture. Although the destruction looked overwhelming and as if it was my dooming end, something in the inside of me would not allow me to lie down and die. It's not what it looks like! There's still work for me to do.

Chapter 9
God's Will

I used to get a little fearful when traveling by airway. One day I chose to meditate prior to take off and I came to terms with the conclusion that I am not in control. I know it sounds like a no-brainer, something that only makes sense but when fear sets in it squeezes every ounce of faith out of oneself. I remember I had to take a trip to Dallas for a work-related conference. I then remembered that I was on the calendar one week from this trip to speak at a Women's Conference on the following Sunday. The understanding was realizing if God had something for me to say to these women at the Women's Conference there was no devil in hell that could stop me from being there. I was going to be there on that Sunday and the only logical way that would happen is if I had a safe trip to and from Dallas. If by chance I didn't make it I can rest assured that absent from the body meant present with the Lord. It may sound small to some but this was a giant revelation to me. It calmed my spirit as I knew without a shadow of a doubt that I had to be at that conference and I was going to be there. When you live by purpose, on purpose for a purpose, all these little fearful stumbling blocks start looking like pebbles. My purpose is greater than any pebble that may come my way. At that point, I could confidently live my life dependent on Jesus Christ and not on anything or anybody else, even myself. Jeremiah 29:11 reads, "For I know the thoughts that I think toward you, saith the Lord, thoughts of peace, and not of evil, to give you an expected end." He already has an expected end for my life, therefore, even if I wanted to die during this entire destruction I would have lived. His will trump's my will. Mind you, God showed up and showed out at that Women's Conference and I am still in awe of how God could use me beyond my own imagination. Guess what, there are even greater things that God has in store for you. You have not reached your full potential. The devil would want you to believe that there's no more elevation for you. You've been doing ministry for 10-20 or more years, you have already preached your best sermon, you have helped all the people you could help but that is an inhibiting spirit that wants to block the works of the one who inhabits you. If you serve a God who sits on a throne in heaven whose earth is his

Theresa Padgett

footstool then what programs your brain to limit what He can do through you. It's time to take the ceiling off of your dreams, your business, your children's destiny. Stop giving up at the bottom of the mountain or for some of us at every pebble or snake thrown in your path.

Another thing, watch out for these snakes. I saw a picture of a bright, vibrant colored snake. There were bright blues, yellows, greens, and reds and the caption read, "Just because it's beautiful doesn't mean it's not poisonous." We can apply that to our interactions in life. Things can appear safe by the naked eye because it looks nice but if you let it too close it can be deadly. You can't put a turd in a box, wrap it with pretty paper and expect me to call it a gift. It is what it is, a turd in a pretty box. Snakes lure you in with their mesmerizing appearance and slivering tongues only to set you up for the bite. The snake has a hidden agenda. Here's some truth, the snake will build you up almost like a dancing cobra moving to your every beat. Saying everything you want to hear then over time alternating compliments with harsh words of venom and actions. Using confusion, deception, and manipulation as a tool because you neglect to use discernment to know if they can be trusted. Telling you how to think or analyze a situation only formulating your brain to their thinking pattern. Usually, the snake wants you to feel safe around them and appear to be on your side. Trying to isolate you from your family, friends, and loved ones, leaving you with no support system ultimately wanting you to be codependent on them. Everybody else is the threat, out to get me, not really my friends according to the snake. However, the truth is that the snake is so low and grimy that they are worried about being exposed. These snakes tend to lose a massive number of people in their lives right before your eyes as they use them and spit them out after squeezing what they need from them through deceiving words and flattering tongues. A leopard never changes its spots, therefore, pay attention to patterns. Likewise, a snake is a snake.

    Be careful of people who act like they made you when they only had the privilege to see how God was developing you. They're going to want dibs on that, trust me. Listen when they say, "You wouldn't have even done that unless I told you." Or "You wouldn't even look like that if it wasn't for me." Be careful who you let kiss you because snakes smell with their tongues. The snake will sniff out the lack of self-value, low self-esteem, or even your pain and weakness. It's beneficial to them that you stay in a position of worthlessness. Once the light comes on and you start coming out the snake will dart away through the nearest hole.

Those who pop into your life when you're going through traumatic experiences seem to only drain and use you for their own personal gain when you're vulnerable and weak. They will only leave you worse off than you were when you first allowed them in. That is not God's will for you. Just like Paul, if bitten by the poisonous snake God will allow you to shake it off into the fire and suffer no ill effects if you remain in him. Even if you come to your senses like the prodigal son after the bite God's grace will restore you.

Wake up, sis. Wake up, brother. I pray the scales fall from your eyes so you won't fall to them that prey on the wounded. I thought at my age people don't operate like this as it is so juvenile and immature. Even at my age, I fell prey during my most vulnerable moment. Repeating the cycle of poor coping mechanisms, creating a false reality, replacing people with people, drowning in ministry, and avoiding self-care not taking the time to heal appropriately. I was completely walking out of the will of God for my life. Be careful when people use scripture to justify your sin, especially when they benefit from it. You are still held accountable for whatever you do in this body. Be mindful of the choices you make and the influences of those around you, especially when you are vulnerable. The enemy sees you and he will use what you like to cause you to stumble. Remember the devil prowls around like a roaring lion looking on whom he may devour.

Gal 5:7-10 also says; "You were running a good race. Who cut in on you to keep you from obeying the truth? That kind of persuasion does not come from the one who calls you. "A little yeast works through the whole batch of dough." I am confident in the Lord that you will take no other view. The one who is throwing you into confusion, whoever that may be, will have to pay the penalty.

Although I walked into this divorce not knowing how it was going to play out I had faith enough to believe that it would work out according to God's perfect plan. My daughter had a hamster named Roger and I used to rant and rave to the children about keeping the cage clean. Finally, she showed us that she could take care of her hamster, so we bought her some toys for Roger. One day my cousin and her family came over and the kids were upstairs playing with Roger. They were watching him roll around in this large plastic ball that you can get from the pet store. They were all eleven and under and there was so much laughter and giggling coming from the room. I urged the children, "Do not take him out of this ball because he could get hurt." They all agreed and continued playing for about 45 minutes. After a while, it got extremely quiet and to my surprise, I heard my daughter crying and her little brother so bravely came marching down the stairs with his shirt off and Roger lying limp in his right hand. He says, "Mom, Mimi took Roger out of the ball and we were trying to take him from her and she squeezed him now he won't move." Her dad grabbed Roger and confirmed, "He is dead" and proceeded to instruct our son to go throw him in the trash outside. Once he went outside he came back in with excitement yelling, "He's alive!" Once he tossed him in the trash, he hit the bottom and he began to run around the bottom of the trash can. Unbelievable, the hamster had every sign of death and we were all convinced that he was dead. Yet, it was his will to live and not die. Your situation may have hit the bottom of the trash but if it is God's will to live, take another look, your situation too can miraculously be revived. I don't care how convincing a situation's outcome may look. I'm here to tell you that it's not over until God says it's over. The bank account may be empty, you may be putting in job application after job application with no callback, the refrigerator is getting low but my God says that He will supply all

Transforming Into Disasters Worst Enemy

of my needs and that He will perfect that thing which concerns you. Sometimes we need to be aware of those in our circle because the naysayers can cloud what God is trying to show us. How do you say that? Well, this test that I am going through I could only go through on my own. This situation was designed to take me to another level and everybody is not going to understand that. When the disciples woke Jesus in the boat He said, "O ye of little faith, why are you afraid," and proceeded to calm the winds and the waves. Some storms come to increase our faith and also reveal to us how much faith we are actually operating. If we listen to the naysayers and other disciples who may not be in the same season as you we tend to adopt the majority's thoughts, ideas, or doubts. In return, repeating the cycle of constantly missing the lesson or the opportunity for growth. Satan will use any opening or crack he can get into, especially when trying to be the doctor for your own sickness. Quite like the human eye and respiratory system in chapter three, how the open gate and easy access to the vital areas of my life left me open and vulnerable to predators. You have the power to close the gate in your life, your children's and spouse's life. You are the gatekeeper at which you need to understand if you build without the Lord it is in vain and if you watch without the Lord it too is in vain.

Theresa Padgett

It's time that I live in perfect peace. How do we yet find perfection as imperfect people? True, all of the arguments are the same: that we were born flawed, born into sin that everything about us is imperfect because we live in an imperfect world. What happens when the perfector shows up? I was told in my bible that all imperfection is made perfect when he shows up. Now, what does that mean? You have to allow the Holy Spirit in your life; therefore, you will have perfect peace that is not equal to this world. Once I was able to wrap my mind around and allow God's heavenly will to touch me here on earth there was no stopping me. I shall live and not die. Remember the exodus is a mass departure of people. Therefore, if I don't come out they won't come out. I have gone beyond surviving but overcoming.

Chapter 10:
Empowerment

I began this book by discussing the resilience of the human body. It was created to live and I used the example of a person who after an autopsy the report indicated that the person had a blockage in one of the blood vessels in the heart but the person never had a heart attack because vessels grew around the blockage to avoid the damage. Quite like the coping mechanisms that I am still working so diligently to completely extinguish. Constantly, after every tragic situation building around the damage to avoid the pain confirms the idea of getting through things by not directly dealing with that issue to make sure they no longer exist. What about you? Are you tap-dancing around certain situations, people, or even yourself to avoid the work? Are you avoiding the blockage? Do yourself a favor, uproot the problem or it will just come back even worse and more than likely at the most inopportune time in your life. Now, was that person's cause of death related to clogged arteries? Who's to say, but if it was a circulatory cause of death the heart attack

Theresa Padgett

may have exposed some necessary health problems that could have been dealt with a long time ago, ultimately avoiding death. Dealing with the damage head-on gives you the power to understand its cause, effects, and ultimately wisdom for yourself and others. Deal with the damage. The effects of not dealing with the damage are even more damaging.

I have learned more things about myself over these last two years of healing than I have my entire life. I've met a girl who needed to be healed from more than this recent incident. My "mother's issues" have polluted my relationship with my children. The inability to understand love has clouded my ability to show love unconditionally and, furthermore, to wholeheartedly forgive. It's a continuous process as every time I think I've conquered forgiveness something occurs to show me that I have not. The lesson keeps repeating in different forms. Recently, after dealing with so much destruction an incident occurred that left me in a situation where I not only needed to forgive but be forgiven. I couldn't sit in my ex-husband's seat until now. How torturing it was for him to keep pleading for my forgiveness and I heartlessly kept ignoring him. Although I was hurt because I dealt with the poor coping mechanisms I can

Transforming Into Disasters Worst Enemy

now sympathize with him. People make horrible choices for so many reasons and it's not the victim's job to work through that person's internal issues but sympathizing allows forgiving to come a little easier. Forgiving with that fake religious forgiveness, saying I forgive because the Bible says if I don't forgive them my father in heaven won't forgive me. Saying it with my mouth but it all being so far from my heart causes me to suffer. I've said true forgiveness occurs when you can talk about the offense and it doesn't hurt anymore. What if you don't talk about it? What if you built a wall to block the damage? This is what the Bible says about the one who needs forgiveness at which I was not concerned about until I needed it.

"If anyone has caused grief, he has not so much grieved me as he has grieved all of you to some extent—not to put it too severely. The punishment inflicted on him by the majority is sufficient. Now instead, you ought to forgive and comfort him, so that he will not be overwhelmed by excessive sorrow. I urge you, therefore, to reaffirm your love for him. Another reason I wrote to you was to see if you would stand the test and be obedient in everything. Anyone you forgive, I also forgive. And what I have forgiven—if there was anything to forgive—I have forgiven in the sight of

Christ for your sake, in order that Satan might not outwit us. For we are not unaware of his schemes." 2 Corinthians 2:5-11 NIV

Constantly living with my heart sheltered with both hands won't let love in nor let love out. Not trusting my reality and creating my own have allowed me to live in a fairy tale world that only exists in the movies. Can admit that some internal issues that I have discovered had a lot to do with my responses, actions, and the force of the traumatic impact resulting in me opening my eyes underneath the rubble. Life is messy. It's not a cookie-cut situation. Everybody is not going to live like I believe they should live. Even though I did not self-inflict pain on myself the level of force from the trauma was increased because I was already living in trauma. Some battles choose us but it does not mean we won't come out on top. So, pity for the battle that so arrogantly chose me or my family. You should have the same confidence in knowing that the enemy can't win a fixed fight.

I have been transformed into disasters' worst enemy. Leaving those ways, bad habits, and old coping mechanisms under the dirt. As Sara Jakes said, "you can't be who you're becoming and who you were at the same time." Had to let the old go and embrace the renewing of my mind. Here's the catch, let God do only what He can do. What was designed to destroy me I now have the formula to destroy but the secret was revealed underneath all of the rubble. That which was supposed to crush me, or cause me to die from hyperthermia, dehydration, and suffocation had no power to destroy what God had already declared will live. No, instead I endured the pressure, maintained my cool, refreshed my thirst with the living water, and inhaled the breath of life a little deeper. Now we get up, dust ourselves off, hold our heads up, and take one step at a time to a new, revived, whole person.

Equipped with consciousness, firepower, and pertinacity you too can use the formula A.T.H20 every time destruction tries to cave in on you. This formula simply reminds you to tap into and concentrate on the air, temperature, water, and not the rubble that you're under. Looking at the rubble causes anxiety and fear that would have no room to exist if your will to live lined up with God's will for you to live. Even right now as I confess that how hard it is to mean that when you're actually under it. You've heard me say time and time again that it is not what it looks like. I may see the destruction but I have to see past the destruction. What did God say? Am I more than a conqueror when I appear to be bleeding on the floor defeated? Absolutely correct! Pressed but not crushed, perplexed but not in despair, persecuted but not abandoned, and finally, cast down but not destroyed. This book is about to be known across the globe as it is connected to awards, accolades, and most of all, real people like you and me. God is going to supernaturally open doors, create opportunities and platforms for me to share with people just like you so you can be empowered through motivational speaking and the Live ATH20 Conferences. Look for one in a town near you soon. The motive is not to have a million survivors but a billion transformed disaster destroyers; an uncountable amount of overcomers!

     In conclusion, I look forward to all of the good things connected to the book but I cannot overlook the most important transformation of my children's lives and our relationship that have been tested and tried through the fire. Just like all impurities are burned off through the fire like refined silver, so are we. Newness in our minds, body, and most of all, our Spirit. All of this had to happen in order for who we really are to be surfaced. Not caked down by what we wanted it to look like but ultimately what God wanted it to look like. Man, this thing called life can be challenging but at the end of the day, it is beautiful to actually live and not just exist. Look out for two more books to be born in relation to some of those burnt impurities, "Love Reborn", a 30-day prayer book, Devotional book and a story that will open the conversation that has been covered up in families for years, "When the Lights Go Out".

As I've walked this journey of healing uncovered over the last 12-18 months with all of you I must say that as I write the last page in this book, with tears in my eyes, the final constraint has fallen. Writing has allowed me to see why some of these lessons keep repeating. What doors that I've left open, what self-created mechanisms I use and, most of all, the false replacements I've used to fill voids in my life and having released the last camouflage burden have freed me to enter my destiny as God has planned. It goes even deeper that I am now understanding the voids and where they are rooted so they may be filled with the appropriate thing which is the Holy Spirit.

Most of you may not even realize that you're faulty behaviors, submerging yourself in your job, ministry, or the unfortunate issue of letting the wrong person in your life has a lot to do with needing to fill a void that you never dealt with. I'm not sure if you're reading this during a time where you need encouragement but remember denial is the first step through the grieving process. Empty areas in our life caused by trauma leave voids that can never be filled without God. As you search for who you are and what it is in you that causes you to think, act or talk the way you do, be like that little toddler who so innocently asks "why." No, Jenny, you can't have candy right now. "Why?" Because it's morning. "Why?" You didn't have breakfast yet. "Why?" The last time I let you eat candy on an empty stomach your tummy started hurting and you threw up all morning, do you remember. "Oh...that's why." If you do that with every bad habit, how you discipline your children, respond to your spouse, unkind responses to strangers, racism, prejudices or even unforgiveness you will be able to deal with the damage ultimately avoiding the relationship death of your family, friends, or co-workers. Now that I am free and empowered, completing this book signifies the introduction of the new me. Hello, my name is Theresa Marie Padgett and I am an amazing, inspiring, talented woman that operates in consciousness, pertinacity, firepower and whose purpose in life is to collaborate with others to empower themselves mentally, emotionally, physically and spiritually. Declaring now that I am out from underneath the rubble I can see that the best is yet to come!

About The Author

Theresa M Padgett RN, OCN is dedicated to collaborating with others to empower themselves spiritually, mentally, physically & emotionally. A transparent, compassionate Christian whom is courageous and unashamed of sharing her personal experiences to help others heal. You have to accept where you came from to know where you're going. Purpose over pain. More than a survivor but a conqueror!

www.ingramcontent.com/pod-product-compliance
Lightning Source LLC
Chambersburg PA
CBHW051435290426
44109CB00016B/1565